Humanization and the
Politics of God

Humanization and the Politics of God

The *Koinonia* Ethics of Paul Lehmann

Nancy J. Duff

WILLIAM B. EERDMANS PUBLISHING COMPANY
GRAND RAPIDS, MICHIGAN

Copyright © 1992 by Wm. B. Eerdmans Publishing Co.
255 Jefferson Ave. S.E., Grand Rapids, Mich. 49503

Printed in the United States of America

Library of Congress Cataloging-in-Publication Data

Duff, Nancy J., 1951-
Humanization and the politics of God: the koinonia ethics of Paul Lehmann /
Nancy J. Duff.
p.   cm.
Revision of the author's thesis (doctoral) — Union Theological Seminary.
Includes bibliographical references.
ISBN 0-8028-0494-2 (pbk.)
1. Lehmann, Paul Louis, 1906-   . 2. Christian ethics — History —
20th century.   I. Title.
BJ1231.D84   1991
241'.0404'092 — dc20
92-4739
CIP

To my husband
David C. Mertz

Contents

Contents

Preface

It has been my privilege over the past eighteen years to count Paul and Marion Lehmann among my friends. In 1974, during the spring semester of my first year as a seminary student at Union Theological Seminary in Virginia, Paul Lehmann taught an introductory course in Christian ethics. Little did I know then that seven years later I would talk to him about my plans to write my dissertation on his work, or that eleven years later he and his wife, Marion, would travel from New York to Texas to take part in my wedding. I will always be grateful that both my professional and my personal life have been graced by the presence of these two remarkable people.

In an earlier form the material that makes up this book was submitted as a doctoral dissertation at Union Theological Seminary in New York City. I am especially grateful to Prof. Christopher L. Morse, who chaired the review committee and directed the dissertation. His capacity for critical thinking and precise expression of ideas has challenged me to press toward ever greater clarity and depth in my own theological work. I am also grateful to Prof. James Cone, who broadened my vision as a theologian by encouraging me to examine worlds not my own. I thank Barbara Hall for traveling from Virginia to New York to add a New Testament perspective to the defense, and Larry Rasmussen for his thoughtful and critical questions. I thank Prof. J. Louis Martyn for his influence, which can be seen throughout this work.

I am grateful to my colleagues at Brite Divinity School in Fort Worth for believing that a systematic theologian would make a good teacher of ethics. In calling me to a position in Christian ethics, they forever changed the direction of my teaching. Furthermore, they suffered gladly (and sometimes not so gladly) a new colleague who was struggling to start her teaching career and finish her dissertation at the same time. I am grateful for their patience. I also wish to express my appreciation for my friends and colleagues at Princeton Theological Seminary, where I now teach and where these pages were (finally) brought to their completion.

I wish to thank Mary Hietbrink of Eerdmans Publishing Company for her incredibly careful reading of the text and astute editorial comments. I also thank Mr. William B. Eerdmans for his encouragement and for his interest in ensuring that Paul Lehmann's work will continue to hold a significant place in the present discussion in Christian ethics. I also thank Michelle J. Bartel, a very capable doctoral student in Christian ethics at Princeton Theological Seminary, for her careful work on the indexes.

I want to express my appreciation for my parents, who have in a variety of ways contributed greatly to my vocation as a seminary professor. Finally, I thank my husband, David C. Mertz, for his ever-persistent support.

Introduction

Paul Lehmann believes that Reformed theology offers perspectives that are vital for the contemporary discipline of Christian ethics. His book on ethical method, *Ethics in a Christian Context,* seeks to show "that the faith and thought of the Reformation provide insights into and ways of interpreting ethics which give creative meaning and direction to behavior."[1] Lehmann's ethic reflects three fundamental tenets of Reformed faith.

1. *The Reformed tradition gives ethics a christological rather than an anthropological focus.* Lehmann himself claims that Christian ethics is "oriented toward revelation and not toward morality"[2] because the initial focus of Christian ethics is on the activity of God in Jesus Christ, and only then, derivatively, on the activity of humanity. Although his ethic emphasizes what it means to be "human," Lehmann never aligns himself with non-theological forms of humanism or with the theological tradition that begins with Christian anthropology. "Humanization" is always a result of God's activity in Jesus Christ, never simply a "natural" outgrowth of human activity.

1. Lehmann, *Ethics in a Christian Context* (New York: Harper & Row, 1963), p. 14.
2. Ibid., p. 45.

1

2. *Reformed thinking gives ethics a "contextual" rather than a prescriptive character and task.* According to Lehmann, the "faith and thought of the Reformation liberate ethical thinking from the abstractness and confinement of principles and precepts," allowing for more "experimental responses" to the humanizing activity of God in the world. God's will is primarily mediated *not* by universal laws but by a contextual understanding of what God is doing "to make and to keep human life human." This does not mean, however, that the circumstances of each isolated situation alone dictate Christian behavior. Rather, divine activity creates the context for decision-making and transforms human behavior.[3] Human beings respond to God's activity so that their actions become living parables of God's action. The function of ethics is to *describe* divine action and human transformation and response.

3. *The Reformers locate the point of departure of Christian ethics in the Christian* koinonia. In the *koinonia,* the community of faith, the political activity of God and its humanizing effect are apprehended. Lehmann takes from Reformed theology an emphasis on the communion of saints, never focusing solely on the individual. While the individual is not ignored or lost in a corporate structure, individual identity and ethical choices are played out in the context of the *koinonia.* For this reason Lehmann replaces the word "moral" with the word "mature" when describing the believer's response to God's activity. Mature Christian behavior focuses not on rules and precepts, as morality does, but on "human relatedness."[4]

The common thread that runs through all three influences from Reformed theology is that Christian ethics begins with the activity of God.[5] Human behavior is always defined in relation

3. Ibid., p. 14.
4. Ibid., p. 15.
5. While Lehmann's ethics shares a common foundation with the theology of the Reformers, he does not hesitate to disagree with the Reformers, sometimes modifying Reformed thought and at other times contradicting it outright. An example of the former is apparent in Leh-

to divine behavior. The two images forming the title of this book
— "humanization" and "the politics of God" — point to Lehmann's emphasis on divine activity. It is *God's* political activity
in Jesus Christ that creates humanizing behavior. In other words,
"humanization" is a direct result of the "the politics of God."
Human behavior is a response to God's activity — a response,
moreover, that becomes a living parable or signification of God's
action. The purpose of this book is to explore and evaluate the
implications of Lehmann's conviction that Christian ethical activity is defined from the perspective of the activity of God. Two
related tasks are necessary to carry out this project.

First, there is the task of defining key concepts in Lehmann's
work. This expository task becomes particularly necessary in
light of the frequent complaint that Lehmann's writing is difficult to understand. Sometimes this complaint is made in response to Lehmann's style of writing, particularly his frequent
use of poetic allusion and foreign phrases. Although he often
traces the etymology of words, he tends not to give precise
definitions; often he relies on the "self-evident" meaning of
words, ideas, and poetic images. This tendency leads some critics to accuse him of being platitudinous, of preferring the flair
of a well-turned phrase to precise definition.

Others find his line of argument traveling in a different
direction than their own logic will allow. Consider: at an ordination service for a woman, Lehmann preached a sermon on
Paul's injunction that women keep silent in the churches; he
has made the seemingly contradictory claim that revolutionary
violence is never justifiable but sometimes necessary; he has
told us that the feminist movement within theology has now

---

mann's move from an exclusive to a more universal understanding of
God's saving activity in the world. An example of the latter is demonstrated in Lehmann's rejection of the first of Calvin's three uses of the law
— that is, Calvin's idea that the law prepares us to receive grace. While
Lehmann is true to the foundations of Reformation thought, he is not
blindly tied to them. He consistently rejects a wooden repetition of the
doctrines of the tradition in favor of a lively conversation that leaves room
for disagreement.

freed us to call God "Father." All these represent angles of argument that infuriate many and simply leave others confused.[6] While Lehmann's train of thought is neither inconsistent nor illogical, his logic often takes him on detours and byroads. While *he* never loses the thread of his argument, always arriving back at the original point, his readers sometimes find themselves lost in what seems like a maze of details, literary allusions, and historical minutiae. This confusion might be exacerbated by Lehmann's writing style, which tends to be dynamic and explosive rather than plodding and methodical.

Nevertheless, it is a mistake to believe that Lehmann gives *no* indication of the meanings of the terms he uses. In what may appear to be a maze of images, there lies illuminating description. Accordingly, some attention will be devoted to uncovering the meanings of Lehmann's terms with the hope that readers will be better able to engage in conversation with Lehmann's work when they have a more thorough and accurate understanding of his position.

The second task involves moving beyond exposition and seeking to analyze three ideas key to Lehmann's method: narrative, apocalyptic, and parabolic action. Further development of these ideas will answer some of Lehmann's critics by clarifying what he means when he claims that "God acts." Examining Lehmann's use of these three concepts and their further development by other scholars will illuminate his approach to ethics sympathetically and critically. I will argue that the relationship between narrative, apocalyptic, and parabolic action gives to Lehmann's ethics the concreteness and specificity that his critics claim are lacking.

To accomplish both the expository and the critical tasks, I will proceed in the following manner:

6. Lehmann expressed his interpretation of the ordination of women in an unpublished sermon he preached on 20 May 1973; he articulates his position on revolutionary violence in *The Transfiguration of Politics* (New York: Harper & Row, 1975), pp. 264-65; his comment regarding the reference to God as "Father" is made in "The Decalogue and a Human Future," an unpublished manuscript that will become his next book.

4

In Chapter One, "Humanization and the Politics of God," I will define three concepts that are essential to understanding Lehmann's ethics: "humanization," "the politics of God," and "the *koinonia*." After defining these terms, I will describe the relationship Lehmann establishes between ethics and human politics.

In Chapter Two, "The Contextual Character of Christian Ethics," I will explore Lehmann's contextual approach to ethics by comparing it with the approaches of others whose ethics have been described as "contextual" or "situational." Thus the positions of Jean-Paul Sartre, Joseph Fletcher, Karl Barth, and Stanley Hauerwas will be compared with Lehmann's contextualism.

In Chapter Three, "Lehmann's Interpretation of Revelation and Story," I will argue that a fuller development of Lehmann's claims for the importance of story will clarify his claims regarding divine action. This chapter will explore Lehmann's use of story in relation to the work of other scholars who have employed the same term.

In Chapter Four, "The Significance of Apocalyptic for Lehmann's Ethics," I will demonstrate that Lehmann's description of divine activity coincides with many of the characteristics of apocalyptic theology found in the letters of the apostle Paul. The apocalyptic themes to be explored are (1) revelation as radically discontinuous with the structures of the world, (2) divine lordship, (3) the inauguration of the New Age, and (4) the imminent parousia.

In Chapter Five, "Public Accountability and Revolutionary Violence," I will first discuss Lehmann's ethics in relation to the contemporary debate over "public accountability." In the second part of this chapter I will seek to demonstrate how Lehmann's ethics guide him in a discussion of a contemporary issue — revolutionary violence.

It is my hope that these pages will serve several groups of people with varying degrees of familiarity with Paul Lehmann's work. First, I hope that this book will serve as an introduction to those who have never read Lehmann's work before. Second, I hope that those who have read Lehmann's work but who have put it aside will return to it once again and rediscover its ongoing significance for the field of Christian ethics. Finally, I hope that those who have over the years continued to rely on Lehmann's work will find reflected in these pages the admiration and respect which so many of us have for Lehmann's distinctive and perceptive approach to theological ethics. In each case I hope that my book will send the reader back to Lehmann's texts eager to enter into lively conversation with him about both the method and the content of his *koinonia* ethic.

I

Humanization and the Politics of God

Paul Lehmann begins his account of ethics with a brief etymology of the word "ethics" in an effort to arrive at its fundamental meaning.[1] According to this history, the Greek root of our word ethics *(to ethos)* originally meant "dwelling" or "stall," and referred, therefore, to the security one provides for animals. The verb form of "ethics" *(iotha)* originally meant "to act according to custom." The Greeks apparently believed that custom provides security for humanity in the same way in which the stall provides security for animals. Although Lehmann's attention is not focused on custom, he believes that our word "ethics" has retained this general idea of stability by focusing on the "stability and security which are necessary if one is going to act at all" (*Ethics,* p. 24).[2] The etymology of the word "ethics," says Lehmann, "points to the germinal idea that 'ethics' is concerned

---

1. Lehmann, *Ethics in a Christian Context* (New York: Harper & Row, 1963), pp. 23-24. All subsequent references to this volume will be made parenthetically in the text. See also Paul Lehmann, "The Foundation and Pattern of Christian Behavior," in *Christian Faith and Social Action,* ed. John A. Hutchison (New York: Charles Scribner's Sons, 1953), p. 97.

2. Lehmann says that "the word 'morality' came gradually to be reserved for behavior according to custom" (see *Ethics,* pp. 24-25).

with that which holds human society together. It is, so to say, the 'cement' of human society, providing the stability and security indispensable to the living of human life" (*Ethics,* p. 25).[3]

In the history of ethics, the source of this stability has been identified in at least two major ways. First, one can identify the law as that which "holds human society together," because the law sets the parameters within which the individual and the community should act. A Christian ethic of law usually focuses on God's commandments as revealed in the Old and New Testaments, but sometimes includes natural and ecclesiastical law as well. According to H. Richard Niebuhr, this approach to ethics locates ethical significance in the identification of the "right" thing to do.[4] In a second approach to ethics, one identifies goals or ideals as providing the stability necessary for responsible human action. In this perspective, ethics judges all human action in relation to a common *telos.* Christian teleological ethics often identifies the *telos* with a key biblical concept — for example, the kingdom of God or *agape.* According to Niebuhr, this teleological approach to ethics locates ethical significance in the identification of the "good" thing to do, the *summum bonum.*[5]

In opposition to these two types of ethics, Lehmann claims that neither laws nor goals provide the necessary security for holding human society together. He believes that the absolute standards of behavior defined by an ethic of law or an ethic of ideals have an abstract quality which removes ethics from the complexities of human life. In keeping with the fundamental meaning of the word "ethics," Lehmann emphasizes the ethical

---

3. Throughout his work Lehmann provides us with such etymological accounts. The reader who may be tempted to skim these accounts quickly in order to return to the heart of Lehmann's argument could overlook important information. Lehmann is not simply providing us with interesting bits of trivia in the history of language. Here, for instance, the concern for "that which holds human society together" and for "the stability and security indispensable to the living of human life" stands at the heart of his approach to ethics.

4. Niebuhr, *The Responsible Self: An Essay in Christian Moral Philosophy* (San Francisco: Harper & Row, 1978), p. 55.

5. Ibid.

significance of the context of human behavior rather than rules or ideals (*Ethics,* p. 347).

The approach Lehmann takes over against teleological and law-oriented ethics shares similarities with what Niebuhr calls "an ethic of response." This approach locates ethical significance in the identification of the "fitting" thing rather than the "right" or the "good" thing — that is, it seeks the fitting response to each particular situation. Thus, one does not initially ask, "What law should I follow?" or "What is my goal?" but simply, "What is going on?"[6]

According to Lehmann, one can know what is going on only by discerning what God is doing in the world. For him, a "fitting response" not only refers to the situation but also is an appropriate response to *God's* action in each situation, an action that can be perceived only in the context of the *koinonia,* the community of faith. Because God's claim upon us is the foundation of our humanity, providing the security indispensable for human action, the basic ethical question, according to Lehmann, is, "Who is our Lord?" — or, in Luther's words, "What does it mean to have a God?"[7]

In addressing this question, Lehmann uses the phrase "the politics of God" to interpret the Reformed doctrine of providence. According to Lehmann, it is God, not humanity, who initially "makes ethics" (in the fundamental meaning of the word), for it is God who establishes and upholds the conditions necessary for the living of human life. It is God's gracious action on our behalf — the politics of God — which leads to what Lehmann calls "humanization." Lehmann claims that by establishing "the security and stability indispensable for human existence," the politics of God "makes and keeps human life human in the world" (*Ethics,* p. 99).

The activity of the believer becomes, in turn, one of grateful response to divine activity. Lehmann identifies this human re-

6. Niebuhr, *The Responsible Self,* p. 67.
7. Lehmann, "Commandments and the Common Life," *Interpretation,* Oct. 1980, p. 345.

sponse as a "sign" or "parable" of God's action. This "sign-character" of human activity indicates that the believer seeks "to express in behavior the fact that the human condition itself is being shaped by the politics of God" (*Ethics*, p. 144). God's gracious action toward us creates human fellowship — that is, it provides the cement of human society. Our action provides an image or parable of that divine action. Thus, in opposition to teleological ethics and to ethics of absolute law, Lehmann proposes that a Reformed Christian ethic analyzes the "environment of decision" so that "the principial foundations and preceptual directives of behavior are displaced by *contextual foundations* and *parabolic directives*" (*Ethics*, p. 347, emphasis in the original).

Lehmann believes that the Christian *koinonia* provides the primary environment of decision for Christians, for here the political activity of God and its humanizing effects are revealed and apprehended. He describes the Christian *koinonia* as the "fellowship-creating reality of Christ's presence in the world" (*Ethics*, p. 49). Lehmann goes so far as to claim that the *koinonia* is the "ethical reality of the Christian faith," for it reveals both the structure of God's activity in the world and the structure of interrelatedness that God in Jesus Christ creates among human beings (*Ethics*, p. 56). This structure indicates that Christ did not come to give a new law or to reveal the *telos* of humanity; Christ came to transform human lives.

The *koinonia* has proleptic significance because it points to the transformation not only of believers but of all humanity. Therefore, when the fundamental meaning of ethics is translated into a theological discipline, the primary concern of Christian ethics becomes "the concrete ethical reality of a transformed human being and a transformed humanity owing to the specific action of God in Jesus Christ" (*Ethics*, p. 17). The Christian *koinonia* offers a foretaste of this divine action and human transformation. This focus on God's action in Jesus Christ, its location within the *koinonia*, and its humanizing effect lead Lehmann to define the theological discipline of ethics as "reflection on the question and its answer 'What am I as a believer in Jesus Christ and a member of his church to do?'" (*Ethics*, p. 25).

The purpose of this study is to examine Lehmann's theological ethics with particular focus on the implications of defining Christian ethical activity from the perspective of divine action. The specific question to be addressed is whether Lehmann's claims for the "contextual foundations" and "parabolic directives" of ethics provide adequate guidance in the making of specific moral choices.

I will argue that the guidance Lehmann provides does *not* require the addition of such concepts as prudence, orders of creation, or middle axioms, as some of his critics claim. Such additions would indeed undermine Lehmann's method for theological ethics. What is required is clarification of what Lehmann means when he says, "God acts." Accordingly, in this book I will focus on Lehmann's concepts of narrative, apocalyptic, and parabolic action, comparing and sometimes augmenting his claims for these concepts with other work in the field in order to provide a better understanding of what he means when he refers to the activity of God. As a means of further describing Lehmann's method, in this opening chapter I will explore three key concepts in Lehmann's ethics — humanization, the politics of God, and *koinonia* ethics — as well as the relation he establishes between ethics and human politics.

Humanization

Lehmann's interest in that environment which provides the stability necessary for holding human life together focuses his attention on the question of what it takes "to make and to keep human life human in the world" (*Ethics,* p. 99). Critics, however, claim that this well-known phrase is imprecise. Believing that the meaning of the word "human" is self-evident, Lehmann finds it unnecessary to give a precise definition.[8] Confu-

8. Lehmann, "On Keeping Human Life Human: A Philosophic Venture into Man's Apperception of the Relation of His Selfhood to the Divine," *Christian Century* 81.2, no. 43 (1964): 1297-99. Lehmann responds to ques-

sion has arisen, however, because three "self-evident" meanings of the word occur in everyday language. First, the word "human" refers to the biological designation of that which belongs to the realm of *homo sapiens* in distinction from the plant and animal world. Second, the word designates that which is negative about human beings, as the maxim "To err is human" and the excuse "I'm only human" imply. Third, the term is used in a way directly opposite to the second usage, to refer to that which is admirable about human nature. Thus we refer to someone as "a real human being" or a *mensch* ("a person of integrity and honor").

Lehmann's understanding of the word encompasses but is not exhausted by these three uses from everyday language. For him the true meaning of the common uses of the word "human" comes to light only when given theological perspective. In the first instance, contrary to what John Macquarrie suggests, Lehmann never uses the word "human" as a strictly biological designation of the species.[9] Rather, when given theological perspective, the biological understanding of "human" requires Lehmann's question to be read, "What is required for human beings to treat one another as those created in the image of God rather than as objects or as animals?" When the second everyday usage — to refer to what is negative about human beings — is given theological reference, the question becomes, "What makes human beings sinful?" The answer to this negative formulation of the question is presupposed whenever Lehmann speaks of "making and keeping human life human." Finally, when the third everyday usage — to refer to that which is admirable about

tions regarding the meaning of the word "human" by quoting an old saying: "If you have to ask the price of something, then you can't afford it." Similarly, if you have to ask what the word "human" means, you're in more serious trouble than you realize. Because of responses like this, critics charge Lehmann with being platitudinous when precise definition is needed. It is not true, however, that we are left with no other assistance from Lehmann than the injunction "Let those who have ears to hear — Hear!" Lehmann tells us that the definition of "human" is understood in light of God's activity in Jesus Christ — that is, in light of the politics of God.

9. Macquarrie, *In Search of Humanity: A Theological and Philosophical Approach* (New York: Crossroad Publishing Company, 1983), pp. 1-2.

human nature — is given theological reference, the question becomes, "What is required to live and act as redeemed children of God?"

These three uses of the word "human," when theologically interpreted, correspond to the three descriptions of humanity that Lehmann claims are affirmed by Christian anthropology: human beings are creatures, sinners, and believers. Lehmann spelled out his interpretation of these three basic affirmations of Christian anthropology in an early series of essays published in 1944 and 1945.[10] He did not, however, include this explication of the doctrine of humanity in *Ethics in a Christian Context,* his book on ethical method published in 1963. This omission has perhaps fueled the criticism that he gives insufficient attention to the definition of "human." Thus a summary of his Christian anthropology from the earlier essays is in order.

In turning to that summary, we should remember that, in Lehmann's view, the affirmations made by Christian anthropology have Christological foundations. As Lehmann points out, the Christian church has never included in its creeds a confession of faith in humanity.[11] Rather, we confess our faith in Jesus Christ, through whom God reveals not only God's self but human identity as well.

Also important to understanding Lehmann's definition of "human" is a clear distinction between the definition of "human" and what is meant by "humanization." A difference exists, for instance, between the claim that human beings are sinners (one aspect of the definition of "human") and the fact that Christ will make us more "human" (a result of "humanization"). The latter reference to humanization does not, of course, mean that Christ will make us more sinful! Rather, the definition of "human" identifies us as creatures; "humanization"

10. Lehmann, "The Christian Doctrine of Man, I: Man as Creature," *The Journal of Religious Thought* 1, no. 2 (1944): 140-56; "The Christian Doctrine of Man, II: Man as Sinner," *The Journal of Religious Thought* 2, no. 1 (1944): 60-77; "The Christian Doctrine of Man, III: Man as Believer," *The Journal of Religious Thought* 2, no. 2 (1945): 179-94.

11. Lehmann, "Man as Creature," p. 141.

brings us back to an active understanding of our origins. The definition of "human" tells us we are sinners; humanization provides the weapons to fight *against* sin. The definition claims we are believers; humanization tells us we are believers not by nature but because Christ leads us to believe.

In all three cases, both the definition of "human" and the process of humanization require the activity of God in Jesus Christ. Both to *know* that we are creatures, sinners, and believers (the definitions of "human") and to *live* as creatures, redeemed sinners, and believers (what we become through the process of humanization) require the action of God in Jesus Christ. Therefore, Lehmann claims that an ethic of messianism rather than an ethic of humanism is required in order to describe how human beings live responsibly. An ethic of messianism is also required to define the opposite of humanization. Dehumanization, according to Lehmann's ethic, results when people are forced to be other than who God intends them to be individually and communally.

So that we might better understand what Lehmann means by "humanization," in what follows I will outline Lehmann's description of human beings as creatures, sinners, and believers.

Human Beings as Creatures. Lehmann points out that we can make the first affirmation of Christian anthropology — namely, that human beings are creatures — only because we have already affirmed that God is Creator; the very designation "creature" indicates that humanity is properly understood only in reference to the Creator, never with reference solely to itself. When one interprets the definition of "human" as *self*-derivatory, one has already set out on the road toward dehumanization, ignoring the truth that humanity, by virtue of its creation, is dependent upon God.[12]

Lehmann believes that the Christian doctrine of the image of God — *imago dei* — focuses one's attention on the affirmation

12. Lehmann believes that theological liberalism led to the "bankruptcy of humanism" whereby we have tried for two centuries to believe in ourselves. See "Man as Creature," pp. 142, 143.

that human beings are creatures.[13] This doctrine sets the parameters for humanity's relationship with God and with the rest of creation by upholding both the uniqueness and the dependence of humanity. Christianity errs whenever it emphasizes one over the other. The first error — overemphasizing humanity's uniqueness — arises from rationalism, which exaggerates the uniqueness of human beings in comparison with other creatures by locating human identity almost exclusively in reason. The second error — overemphasizing humanity's dependence — arises from naturalistic interpretations of creation that mitigate the uniqueness of human beings in comparison with other creatures by locating human identity almost exclusively in nature.[14]

Lehmann is especially concerned to guard against the error of rationalism. According to the rationalistic approach, the image of God is an attribute of rational beings and is, therefore, common to both God and humanity.[15] Thus the rationalistic approach interprets the *imago* primarily as a category of being, identifying it with the basic structure of human makeup, particularly the attribute of rationality. This interpretation supports the claim for a structural similarity between the natures of human and divine being. Specifically, the structural similarity is located in the characteristic of rationality.[16]

Lehmann believes that the New Testament disavows the

13. For further discussion of the *imago dei*, see Chapter VI and Appendix B of Ray Anderson's *On Being Human: Essays in Theological Anthropology* (Grand Rapids: Wm. B. Eerdmans, 1982); Emil Brunner, *Man in Revolt: A Christian Anthropology* (New York: Charles Scribner's Sons, 1939); Karl Barth, *Church Dogmatics,* 4 vols. (Edinburgh: T. & T. Clark, 1936-1969), III/1: 183-206; G. C. Berkouwer, *Man: The Image of God* (Grand Rapids: Wm. B. Eerdmans, 1962); and Dietrich Bonhoeffer, *Creation and Fall* (London: SCM Press, 1959).

14. Lehmann, "Man as Creature," pp. 144-45.

15. Ibid., p. 147.

16. This tradition tended to make a distinction between being made in "God's image" *(imago dei)* and being made in "God's likeness" *(similitudo)*. The first denotes a structural identity that remains intact after the Fall; the second refers to our responsible existence before God, which has been destroyed and requires grace for restoration. Most Hebrew scholars today say that this distinction is not valid.

conception of the *imago* as an attribute of rationality. Christologically interpreted, the *imago* indicates not a structural similarity between God and humanity but a relation.[17] Interpreted relationally, the *imago* becomes a dynamic event — that is, the event "of having been called into being by God's Word."[18] Being made in the image of God marks a difference between humanity's relation to God and the other creatures' relation to God. Only humanity was *called* into being, and thus only humanity's existence can be understood as a vocation.[19]

According to this Christological interpretation, we understand that we were created in the image of God only from the standpoint of reconciliation in Jesus Christ. Lehmann finds the Christological focus of the *imago* in New Testament references to the *imago* which emphasize that human beings are children of God in relation to the divine sonship of Christ.[20] Therefore,

17. "Lehmann, "Man as Creature," p. 148. Emil Brunner, Dietrich Bonhoeffer, and Karl Barth also interpret the *imago* as a relationship rather than an attribute.

18. Ibid., p. 153.

19. See Karl Barth's observation regarding the difference between God's command to human beings and God's command to the animals (*Church Dogmatics*, III/4: *The Doctrine of Creation*).

20. Lehmann, "Man as Creature," pp. 153, 149. See also Brunner's *Man in Revolt*, p. 92. Lehmann does not emphasize the two New Testament passages that directly express the *imago*: 1 Corinthians 11:7 ("For a man ought not to have his head veiled, since he is *the image and reflection of God;* but woman is the reflection of man" — emphasis mine) and James 3:9 ("With it [the tongue] we bless the Lord and Father, and with it we curse those who are made in *the likeness of God*" — emphasis mine).

Instead, he refers to the following passages: Romans 8:29 ("For those whom he foreknew he also predestined to be conformed to *the image of his Son,* in order that he might be the first-born within a large family" — emphasis mine); 2 Corinthians 3:18 ("And all of us, with unveiled faces, seeing the glory of the Lord as though reflected in a mirror, are being *transformed into the same image* from one degree of glory to another; for this comes from the Lord, the Spirit" — emphasis mine); Ephesians 4:24 (". . . and to yourselves with the new self, created *according to the likeness of God* in true righteousness and holiness" — emphasis mine); and Colossians 3:9-10 ("Do not lie to one another, seeing that you have stripped off the old self with its practices and have clothed yourselves with the new self, which is being renewed in knowledge according to *the image of its creator*" — emphasis mine).

rather than indicating a category of being, the *imago* indicates a relationship (human beings as children of God) — a relationship, moreover, that demands "responsible existence before God."[21]

Human Beings as Sinners. The *imago dei* sets the stage for the second claim of Christian anthropology — that is, human beings are sinners. In relation to the *imago,* original sin is understood to mean that the capacity for a responsible answer to the "response-demanding" call of God has been distorted. According to Lehmann, a fundamental concern of theology lies in the contradiction of human existence expressed in the concepts of the image of God on the one hand and of original sin on the other.[22] This contradiction can be expressed in two ways.

One way of expressing it is to say that we do not live as we have been created to live.[23] We are created in the image of God (called to be responsible before God), and yet by virtue of original sin we are unable to respond. We attempt to take over our own existence apart from God, thereby denying our true nature. A second way to express the contradiction of human existence is to say that we as human beings sin by necessity and yet are responsible for sin. Sin, which determines our existence in ways beyond our control, is at the same time something for which we are responsible.

Lehmann believes that theology has, since the Reformation, fallen into the error of overemphasizing either the necessity of sin or humanity's responsibility for sin. The theology of the Reformers fell into the error of overemphasizing the necessity of sin. In their zeal against any form of Pelagianism, the Reformers came close to leaving no room for human responsibility.[24] Nineteenth-century liberal theology, however, fell into the error of overemphasizing humanity's responsibility for sin.

21. Lehmann, "Man as Creature," p. 154.
22. This is the same contradiction that we encounter in the negative and positive meanings of the concept "human" which were discussed earlier.
23. Lehmann, "Man as Creature," p. 155.
24. Ibid., p. 75.

When sin is viewed as something for which humanity is totally responsible, it becomes something that can be easily brought under control.

In reaction against nineteenth-century liberalism, Lehmann rejects any positive assessment of human autonomy. He believes that sin is a dynamic force that takes humanity captive and yet is a force for which humanity is in part responsible.[25] It is a corruption of human nature that leads to dehumanization — that is, to activity that denies people the vocation to which God has called them.[26] Therefore, Lehmann believes that Christian thought properly interprets human beings not primarily as "rational animals" but as "fallen creatures." At the same time, Lehmann wants to avoid the error of giving humanity an excuse for its sinfulness by overemphasizing the necessity of sin. Humanity, he claims, remains dependent on and therefore responsible to God; otherwise the *imago* would have been completely destroyed. "The man whose creatureliness is marked by the image of God and who, therefore, has his existence from God and in God," he points out, "has actually altered this position without removing its claim upon him."[27]

Human Beings as Believers. In turning to the third affirmation of Christian anthropology, Lehmann describes two alternatives to living by faith: living by fate and living by folly.

To live by fate is to succumb entirely to the sense of being captive. One believes that human beings are so involved in forces over which they have no control that little significance is ascribed to human action. The belief that one is so tightly bound to the chain of circumstance that what one does can change nothing places little or no responsibility on human action for the contradiction of human existence. Lehmann says this fatalistic spirit finds its severest expression in the Greek tragedies. In them life is understood to have "depth but no meaning." Although one does not seek to escape the world by assuming an attitude of apathy,

25. Ibid., p. 69.
26. Lehmann, "Man as Believer," p. 181.
27. Ibid.

the very pursuit of action ends in tragedy: "What a man does has the positive but fateful significance of involving him more inextricably in the very situation from which he struggles to be free."[28] While seeking to engage in responsible action, one is caught between the vitalities of life and the laws of life without knowing where the center of life lies.

To live according to folly, on the other hand, is to exaggerate the sense of human responsibility to such an extent that human action is given too much significance. One assumes that what one does can change everything. Human action can on its own resolve the contradiction in human experience. This optimistic position trusts humanity to participate in what it believes to be the inevitability of progress. According to Lehmann, this position substitutes faith in humanity itself for faith in the living God.[29] Thus, if the fatalistic view understands life to have "depth but no meaning," folly understands life to have "zest but no depth."

Of these two alternatives to faith, Lehmann believes that living by folly is the more dangerous for humanity and the one that better describes the choice of the modern world.[30] Using Hitler as an example, Lehmann explains why he believes that living by folly is a worse error than living by fate:

> The utopian dreams of a man [Hitler] whose emancipation from all transcendental authority seems a sufficient guarantee of their fulfillment have ended in the nihilistic delirium of a tyrannical state. . . . The spectacle of the most highly cultured

28. Ibid., pp. 185-86.
29. Ibid., p. 186.
30. In contrasting these alternatives, fate and folly, Lehmann says, "The one looks characteristically backward, the other characteristically forward; the one is principally pessimistic, the other is principally optimistic; the one sees no egress from an inexorable chain of circumstance, the other sees egress in an inevitable sequence of progress; the one is tragic, the other, utopian. If one may risk a certain oversimplification, one may say that the mind of antiquity was dominated on the whole by the idea of fate and that the mind of modernity is dominated on the whole by the idea of folly" ("Man as Believer," p. 185).

19

nation of modern times ruined by the most refined barbarism of all times proves nothing so much as that the automatic progress of a robot is a more grotesque illusion than the tragic hero of an ineluctable necessity.[31]

The easy conscience of a world living "in praise of folly" leads humanity to believe that it can become its own lord and that it does not, therefore, need God.

Lehmann holds that the only alternative to living by fate or folly is to live by faith.[32] By "faith" Lehmann does not mean assent to doctrine or acquisition of a certain type of knowledge or feeling; he means "a way of living." By so defining faith, he means to underscore the character of faith as trust in God.[33] Faith is a relationship with God in which human beings acknowledge and live by their dependence on God. If sin is striving toward autonomy, faith is living in relationship. Sin places us in isolation; faith places us in community, relating us to God and to one another.

Lehmann's description of the two alternatives to faith and his understanding that faith involves humanizing relationships with God and with one another stands at the heart of his method for theological ethics. His theology always focuses on community. Human beings were created to live in community with God

31. Ibid., p. 188.

32. In this early essay Lehmann employs a concept that he later abandons: the concept of the guilty conscience. Here he asserts that the broken relationship between God and humanity is "transmitted as guilt" ("Man as Believer," p. 184). The guilty conscience, in turn, becomes the "acute experiential form" of the contradiction between the the image of God and original sin ("Man as Believer," p. 180). Lehmann also claims that the despair produced by this contradiction leads to faith. When the human contradiction between what we can be and what we are leads us to despair, there faith arises. In his later work Lehmann gives up both the idea of the guilty conscience and the notion that human despair leads us to believe. Whereas in his early essays he comes close to suggesting that human beings have a natural capacity to apprehend God, he emphatically denies such a suggestion in his later work. What remains constant in his work is the claim that faith is a "way of living."

33. Ibid., p. 190.

and with one another — hence the *imago dei*. Sin has caused human beings to destroy that community by living in dehumanizing relations with one another. Faith leads to the restoration of that community and thus to the restoration of true humanity.

Given Lehmann's emphasis on humanization, it would be natural for him to attempt to work out his ethics from a well-developed theological anthropology. However, he consistently maintains that while humanization, or the new humanity, is the goal of ethical reflection, Christology is its foundation.[34] His understanding of the nature of humanity implied in the question "What does it take to make and to keep human life human?" requires for its answer a theology of messianism. It is, he claims, the political activity of God centered in Jesus Christ that defines what it means to be human.

The Politics of God

Lehmann tells us that "it is possible to say that God, if he is denotable by one phrase more characteristically than by another, is a 'politician'" (*Ethics*, p. 83). Because a politician is often thought of as someone who makes deals, compromises truth for personal gain, and holds forth empty promises, the claim that "God is a politician" can appear to be a dubious assertion that undercuts rather than illuminates the integrity of divine action. In describing the "politics of God," however, Lehmann is not referring to images of elected officials or the structures of the state and then by analogy applying these images to divine activity. According to Lehmann, "These images, although they are indirectly and ultimately also related to the political character of the divine activity, do not give the primary and direct sense of what the phrase 'God of politics' means." Just as with the word "human," the true meaning of "politics" comes to light only from a theological perspective (*Ethics*, p. 83). In short, when describing the political character of divine activity, Lehmann is not referring primarily to the connota-

34. Ibid., p. 119.

tions of "politics" in its everyday sense; he is using the word in a more fundamental sense. The definition is provided by Aristotle; its specific content is provided by the Bible.

Aristotle defines politics as the science of the supreme Good and ethics as one branch of that science. This science studies the fundamental nature of humanity, for it seeks to discover that form of communal association which most enhances the quality of human life. According to Aristotle, the "city- state" or "polis" creates and enhances the good life. Lehmann summarizes Aristotle's viewpoint this way: "Politics, as Aristotle saw it, is the 'science of the polis'; and the 'polis,' although concretely it is the 'city-state,' is always also the ideal form of human association which is 'by nature' the precondition for and the expression of the fulfillment of human life." Thus, according to Lehmann, the Aristotelian definition of politics leads us to understand that politics (similar to ethics) is "activity, and reflection upon activity which aims at and analyzes what it takes to make and to keep human life human in the world" (*Ethics,* pp. 84-85). Accordingly, politics has fundamentally to do with "the foundations, structures and ends of human community." In short, politics is "community-creating life."[35] It is not Aristotle, however, but the Bible that describes community-creating life. It is the biblical description of divine politics that tells us "what it takes to make and to keep human life human."

Lehmann's primary justification for defining God's activity in political terms lies in the fact that the "formative biblical images" which describe divine activity are "political" in both the fundamental and the everyday uses of that term. These biblical images include references to a chosen "people" delivered from "slavery" and living in "covenant relation." These people are given "laws," "judges," "prophets," and "kings" (*Ethics,* pp. 90-91). The New Testament proclaims that the most significant political image is that of the Messiah (*Ethics,* p. 94). Christ is

35. Lehmann, "The Foundation and Pattern of Christian Behavior," pp. 94-95. In referring to Aristotle, Lehmann's only intention is to provide the fundamental definition of politics. Lehmann rejects Aristotle's specific picture of what the *polis* would look like, including Aristotle's claim that slavery is part of the natural order.

described as the messianic "king" who rules over "principalities and powers," inaugurates the "New Age," and establishes the "kingdom of heaven." Thus the Bible itself uses political images to describe God's activity (*Ethics,* p. 95).

According to Lehmann, however, the significance of these political images is lost when they become part of a list extracted from the biblical story that ties them together. Only in their narrative form do these political images illuminate God's action in the world (*Ethics,* p. 95). The biblical narration of God's political activity describes the constancy of God's movement on behalf of creation. The biblical story is "political" in the fundamental sense of the word because it describes that action which creates humanizing relationships in human community.

This biblical story describes God's movement on behalf of humanity, a movement from creation to redemption to sanctification. It is this divine movement which provides the theological perspective that identifies human beings as creatures, sinners, and believers. First, the story of creation signifies that God wills to be in communion with humanity and that God created and sustains a world "fit to be human in." Thus the biblical story provides the clue that human beings are to treat one another as creatures formed in the image of God. Second, the biblical narration gives an account of human sin in which human beings have broken communion with God and one another, preferring self-definition and the will to subdue the neighbor.[36] Thus the biblical story provides the clue to what makes human beings sinful. Finally, the biblical story gives an account of redemption in Jesus Christ, an account in which human beings are adopted as children of God. Thus the biblical story provides the clue to what is required for human beings to live and act as believers, redeemed and sustained in Jesus Christ (*Ethics,* p. 95). Accord-

36. According to Lehmann, "God's will to fellowship is displaced by man's will to power; and in consequence man has lost the secret of his humanity and the key to the meaning of his life and of the world in which he cannot help but live it out" (*Ethics,* p. 96).

ing to Lehmann, this story of God's movement in Jesus Christ on behalf of creation defines who we are and what we are to do. Lehmann's understanding of this political activity of God grounds theology in Christology and leads him to describe his ethic as an "ethic of messianism."

Although Lehmann claims that one can understand human responsibility only from the perspective of God's revelation in Christ, he never gives us a fully developed Christology. Nevertheless, contrary to what some of his critics have claimed, it is not true that he gives no account of his Christology at all. The doctrine of the Second Adam provides the clearest expression of the Christological foundations of Lehmann's ethics.

Lehmann accepts Karl Barth's claim that the Second Adam, Jesus Christ, is "the norm of all anthropology." From his reading of the fifth chapter of Romans, Barth claims that humanity's "essential and original nature is to be found . . . not in Adam but in Christ. . . . Adam can therefore be interpreted only in the light of Christ and not the other way round."[37] In other words, we understand what it means to be human by looking at Jesus Christ. In Christ we find not the "ideal man" but the revelation of the "new humanity." According to Lehmann, Barth's interpretation of the doctrine of the Second Adam lays the foundation for two important aspects of his own theological and ethical method.

First, when the Second Adam, interpreted as the revelation of true humanity, is used as the foundation for ethics, there is no further recourse to an anthropological foundation. An ethic grounded in anthropology attempts to demonstrate the intelligibility of the ethical demand by presupposing a natural human ability to fulfill the demand. Such an ethic claims that although this natural capacity was corrupted by sin, Christ's saving work brings about its restoration. In this process from "natural capacity" to "corrupted capacity" to "restored capacity," Lehmann believes that the work of Christ loses significance: "If one could

37. Ibid., p. 119. Lehmann is quoting Barth's *Christ and Adam* (New York: Harper & Row, 1957), pp. 26, 29.

be almost as good without Christ as with him, he seem[s] scarcely worth loyalty, or even attention." Whenever one claims that humanity has a natural capacity to triumph over evil, Christ's significance is diminished (*Ethics,* pp. 120-21). Like Barth, Lehmann identifies humanity not with the First Adam but with the Second Adam (Christ), thereby avoiding all reference to natural capacities.

The doctrine of the Second Adam also indicates that the goal of ethical action is the new humanity (*Ethics,* p. 119). For Lehmann, however, this does not mean that Christian behavior is judged against the standard of ideal humanity:

> It has already been remarked that Christian ethics is primarily concerned not with the good but with the will of God; it aims at maturity, not at morality. The theological reasons for this shift are now apparent. The immediate and direct theological presuppositions of Christian ethics have to do with the context and actuality of the new humanity in Christ, not with humanity in general, humanity apart from Christ. (*Ethics,* p. 121)

Lehmann's ethic never analyzes Christian acts against a definition of an ideal. Such an analysis, he believes, can rationally identify responsible behavior but cannot identify what is specifically Christian about behavior (*Ethics,* p. 122). Lehmann's claim that the new humanity provides the goal of ethical action should be understood in light of his definition of faith. Lehmann believes that faith is a way of living; more precisely, it is living in trustful relationship with God, who in Christ calls us into community with one another. This way of living allows us to "see" the world in a particular way and then live out what we see. What we see is the image of God in Jesus Christ, who marks the inauguration and consummation of the new humanity and who calls us to be living parables of the community for which we were created. "The Christian interpretation of behavior," says Lehmann, "starts with and stays within the context of the fact of the new humanity" (*Ethics,* p. 122). Our behavior is to be a "fragmentary foretaste" of its fulfillment. This fragmentary foretaste is located within the Christian community of faith, within the *koinonia*.

The *Koinonia*

The church is created by God's political activity and provides the context in which believers respond to God's activity. Lehmann identifies four important aspects of the *koinonia* according to his reading of the New Testament book of Ephesians.

First, the *koinonia* focuses our attention on human related-ness (*Ethics*, pp. 85, 49). Lehmann points out that the Reformers did not, as is often assumed, bring to theology an emphasis on individualism. Their emphasis on community is evident in the various ways in which they employed the word "communion." "Communion of Saints," the "sacrament of communion," and "to communicate" all point to the idea that the wholeness of each person is tied to the wholeness of all. To go to communion means, in Martin Luther's phrase, "through love being changed into each other." Calvin expressed a similar sentiment when he claimed that "if we wish to belong to Christ, let no man be anything for himself: but let us all be whatever we are for each other." Lehmann wants to recapture the Reformers' emphasis on the community for Christian ethics today: "We are what we are in and through God's action in Christ, bringing our authentic humanity to pass through authentic belonging. Our being at all, our being what we are, is our being in this community. This is the *communio sanctorum*, the fellowship of Christians, in the world" (*Ethics*, pp. 65-66).

According to Lehmann, the Reformers' affirmation of community challenges the American tendency to glorify the "rugged individual" by speaking instead of the "redeemed individual." The image of the "redeemed individual" indicates that while salvation is personal, it is never private, for the redeemed individual does not exalt the idea of "making it on one's own" but recognizes the liberating dependency involved in being a member of the community of faith (*Ethics*, p. 57). The *koinonia*, therefore, guards against two dehumanizing courses of action: the error of disproportionately exalting the individual, as in revivalistic pietism, and the error of disproportionately abasing the individual, as in political totalitarianism (*Ethics,* p. 58).

Lehmann locates a second characteristic of the *koinonia* in "the dialectic between the spiritual and empirical reality of the body of Christ" (*Ethics,* p. 50). Here he stands between those who want to identify the true church with the institutional church and those who claim that the New Testament image of the church has *nothing* to do with an institution. That he does not give the church over to the dangers of institutionalization is evident when his critics claim that his descriptions of the *koinonia* do not match what one experiences the institutional church to be. However, Lehmann does not want to so spiritualize the church that it has no historical form at all. The separation of the *koinonia* from *any* institutional form can lead to an understanding of the church as an *experience* of communion or as an ideal community with no visible form. This more idealistic understanding of the church would be inconsistent with Lehmann's understanding of ethics as "concrete" and "contextual." Lehmann, therefore, proposes that the hidden reality of the *koinonia* and the empirical reality of the church are to be held in tension:

> The *koinonia* is neither *identical* with the *visible* church nor separable from the visible church. *Ecclesiola* in *ecclesia,* the little church within the church, the leaven in the lump, the remnant in the midst of the covenant people, the *koinonia* in the world — this is the reality which is the starting point for the living of the Christian life and for our thinking about Christian ethics. (*Ethics,* p. 72)

Lehmann maintains his starting point for ethical reflection as God's revelation in Jesus Christ; it is a revelation, however, that is always understood in embodied form.

Lehmann identifies the third characteristic of the *koinonia* as the church's diverse gifts. "There is no uniformity, no monotony, in the *koinonia*," he declares. "These diverse gifts are themselves part of the Creator's purpose according to which Christ functions in the world" (*Ethics*, p. 52). It is through diverse gifts that Christ makes known the presence of God in the world. The church, therefore, celebrates diversity among human beings rather than allowing diversity to become an occasion for oppression.

The fourth characteristic of the *koinonia* lies in its recognition that human maturity is a direct result of God's humanizing action in Jesus Christ (*Ethics*, p. 52). Recognizing that the term "maturity" is associated with the field of psychology, Lehmann inverts the psychoanalytic understanding of maturity as "self-realization through self-acceptance" to coincide with the New Testament understanding of maturity as "self-acceptance through self-giving." In so doing, he equates maturity with the biblical concept of "the new humanity" bestowed by Christ (*Ethics*, p. 17). This emphasis on the social character of the self illuminates Lehmann's rejection of both an ethic of ideals and an ethic of law, for he believes that ethics is "concerned with relations and functions, not with principles and precepts" (*Ethics*, p. 124). He believes that maturity can be developed only through interrelatedness, where the wholeness of the individual is located in the wholeness of all (*Ethics*, p. 65).

According to Lehmann, the *koinonia* is the context out of which Christians reflect on God's activity; they are, however, reflecting on God's activity in the world. Thus such theological reflection on the politics of God always leads believers to reflect theologically on *human* politics as well.

Ethics and Human Politics

Early in Lehmann's career his work was described as leaning to the right theologically and to the left politically (*Ethics*, p. 94). The description is still accurate today. Lehmann leans to the theological right in his belief that the traditional Reformed doctrines of the church can add insight to the direction of Christian behavior. He warns that anyone "who wishes to say more than the historic forms of Christian thought seem to allow, [should] look to it that he does not say less than the character of the relations between God and man in Christ requires." While Lehmann insists that "a vital Christian dogmatics will always say things differently," he believes that "it will always be concerned to say the same thing."[38]

Lehmann does not, however, wish to allow dogmatics to maintain the "wooden creedalism" that adherence to the Reformed tradition has often bred. He believes that proper interpretation of the church's doctrines leads to an understanding of the inseparability of theology and ethics and thus to the inseparability of theological ethics and politics. Lehmann's political leaning to the left is a direct result of his understanding of God's activity in the world.

Given his insistence that ethics and politics are bound "inseparably together in authentic Christian behavior,"[39] Lehmann wants to demonstrate that as a theological discipline, Christian ethics does not require a "flight from history." He recognizes that theology has often fallen into the same error Karl Marx charged against philosophy: that it focuses its attention on a variety of *interpretations* of the world without seeking to *change* the world.[40] Lehmann, however, is always concerned to connect patterns of Christian behavior with the concrete conditions of everyday life. As he sees it, the aim of theology is not simply to interpret the world but to connect Christian faith and action in such a way that one enhances the "community-creating function" of politics.[41]

It is important to keep in mind that Lehmann works with

38. Lehmann, "Man as Creature," p. 142.

39. Lehmann, "The Foundation and Pattern of Christian Behavior," p. 96.

40. Lehmann, "Christian Theology in a World in Revolution," in *Openings for Marxist-Christian Dialogue,* ed. Thomas W. Ogletree (New York: Abingdon Press, 1968), p. 100.

41. Lehmann, "The Foundation and Pattern of Christian Behavior," p. 95.

two different definitions of politics — one fundamental, the other consistent with common usage. As we have seen, he takes his fundamental definition from Aristotle, who defined politics as the science of human association — that is, the search for that communal structure which most enhances human life. Lehmann sees politics thus defined as connected with ethics, since divine activity is what allows for human association: it is God who creates and sustains the conditions, environment, and stability necessary for human behavior. Besides using "politics" in this fundamental sense, Lehmann also uses the word in its more everyday sense in references to human governments, laws, agencies, or any structure of power.

As we have seen, Lehmann's interest in the fundamental meaning of politics does not lead to an ethic of moral idealism. With his focus on the "politics of God," he never sets out to describe the "perfect" form of human association whereby all "real" states are judged.[42] He will not allow theological ethics to establish itself in the rift between the "perfect" and the "real." Although the fundamental meaning of "politics" has to do with the ideal form of human association, he insists that theological ethics must not abandon issues of power, oppression, and tyranny, the political problems of a real and flawed world. Lehmann's hope is that the fundamental and the everyday worlds of politics will coincide.

By definition, the "politics of God" is the point at which the two types of politics do coincide. God's political activity always takes on concrete historical form. It is not an abstract ideal toward which we strive but a real movement within the history of the world in which we are called to participate. The fundamental definition of politics describes *God's* activity, but it is always God's activity *in the world* and thus makes an immediate impact on day-to-day politics. By "making and keeping human life human," God draws us into communion with God's self and calls us into communion with one another.

Theological ethics never focuses on "formal doctrinal con-

---

42. See also Lehmann, *The Transfiguration of Politics* (New York: Harper & Row, 1975), p. 29.

siderations" divorced from the everyday "stuff" of human existence. Whereas human politics often destroys humanizing activity, the politics of God creates the environment for humanization. Lehmann claims that God is "breaking in and breaking
up the establishment" in order "to make time and space make
room for human freedom and fulfillment."[43] The politics of God,
he says, creates a transfiguration of human politics that leads to
humanization. The task of Christian ethics is to discern and
describe where God is at work in the world; the church's task
is to join God there.

One important criticism of the connection Lehmann makes
between the politics of God and human politics comes from
James Cone. Like Lehmann, Cone believes that one speaks of
responsible human action by first speaking of the action of God.
However, Cone charges that Lehmann falls short of identifying
the action of God and the central concern of ethics with the
liberation of the oppressed. According to Cone, Lehmann's error
lies in following the Reformers more closely than the Bible:

> Though Lehmann must be given credit for calling theology
> and ethics back to its christological base, he did not carry that
> point to its logical conclusion. He stops short of saying what
> must be said in order to remain faithful to the biblical story:
> namely, that God is not simply the God of politics but the God
> of the politics of the oppressed, liberating them from
> bondage.[44]

Lehmann's emphasis on the community-creating reality of Jesus
Christ is not specific enough for Cone. While one can claim
that Lehmann's understanding of *koinonia*, humanization, and
the politics of God encompasses the liberation of the poor, Cone
wants this concern more specifically spelled out.

In his response to Cone, Lehmann acknowledges that an
exploration of the truth of Christian theology demands that one

43. Ibid., pp. 84, 226.
44. Cone, *God of the Oppressed* (New York: Seabury Press, 1975),
p. 202.

begin with black theology.[45] He accepts the validity of Cone's complaint that *Ethics in a Christian Context* did not address the plight of those who are victims of racism. Further, he acknowledges his debt to Cone for pushing him to address the African-American situation in *The Transfiguration of Politics*.[46]

The similarity and difference between Cone and Lehmann may shed some light on Lehmann's ethics. The similarity lies in Lehmann's understanding that God's action results in humanization and Cone's understanding that God's action results in liberation. Given their definitions of these terms, "humanization" and "liberation" are synonymous. That God's action liberates human beings from oppression is not a point of contention between these two theologians. The major difference between them lies in Lehmann's lack of specificity about whose humanization or whose liberation is at stake. While Lehmann does speak to the specifics of oppression, he does not *begin* with reference to a specific oppressed community. Furthermore, his

45. Lehmann, "Black Theology and 'Christian' Theology," *Union Seminary Quarterly Review* 31, no. 1 (Fall 1975): 31-37.

46. Lehmann's interpretation of Cone's work avoids the shallow responses of many of Cone's critics. For instance, Lehmann recognizes that Cone's use of "black" must be interpreted both literally, as a reference to people of color, and symbolically, as a reference to *all* people who suffer. Furthermore, given his acceptance of Calvin's claim that theological reflection can begin with God or with humanity, Lehmann avoids the angry reaction of some critics to the fact that Cone begins his theological reflection with black experience. Lehmann does point out, however, that "the 'truth' to which 'Christian' theology is open and obedient is not unqualifiedly identical with the concrete reality of blackness or any other concrete reality of the human condition and the human story." Lehmann says that while black theology is Christian theology, Christian theology is not black theology, but in making this distinction he does not mean to suggest that Cone's theology is unchristian; he intends to warn against equating any theology with the transcendent truth to which it speaks. By Lehmann's definition, Christian theology can never be equated with any one theological endeavor. Cone, of course, never intends to make this identification between black theology and the transcendence to which Christian theology points. Although his style is prone to hyperbole, he does not in the end turn the symbolic idea that "God is black" into the idolatrous idea that "black is God" (ibid., p. 32).

poetic phrases sometimes obscure rather than clarify the specific references demanded by Cone. However, Lehmann does intend such specificity in his description of ethics as "contextual," a concept that will occupy our attention in Chapter Two.

II

The Contextual Character
of Christian Ethics

Contextualism

The use of general rubrics to categorize various "schools" of thought creates a dilemma for systematic theology. For instance, to differentiate seventeenth-century "orthodoxy" from nineteenth-century "liberalism" and twentieth-century "neo-orthodoxy" initially provides clear theological demarcations in the history of dogmatics. On closer examination, however, one discovers that very different positions can be categorized under any given rubric. While refraining from using such theological rubrics would add a burden of extreme specificity to theological debate, the clarity gained would perhaps be worth the effort. At the same time, however, we cannot ignore the existence of certain movements within the history of theology that involve challenges and counter-challenges between *groups* of theologians. The best theologian writes not as an isolated individual but as a representative of a particular way of thinking shared by some and not shared by others.

We face this problem of theological rubrics when we encounter the term "contextual ethics." It cannot be denied that there is a distinct debate in theological ethics which arose (in the 1950s) between what James Gustafson calls "roughly de-lineated parties." On one side of the debate are those who defend the use of universal and absolute principles for moral decision-making. On the other side are those who disavow the use of absolute laws or principles and emphasize response to particular situations.[1] The latter position, when considered from this broader perspective, is called "contextualism."[2]

We find, however, vastly different positions grouped together under this single rubric. For instance, placing Paul Lehmann's *koinonia* ethic and Joseph Fletcher's utilitarian ethic under the rubric "contextualism" is highly deceptive. So great are the differences found under this rubric that Gustafson has convincingly argued that the "context-vs.-principles" argument is "a misplaced debate in Christian ethics."[3] Gustafson believes that the debate has ceased to be fruitful because "the umbrella named 'contextualism' has become so large that it now covers persons whose views are as significantly different from each other as they are different from some of the defenders of 'principles.'"[4]

Lehmann himself agrees that the term "contextualism" represents diverse views:

1. Gustafson, "Context vs. Principles: A Misplaced Debate in Christian Ethics," *Harvard Theological Review* 58, no. 2 (Apr. 1965): 171. For a historical account of this debate, see Edward Leroy Long, Jr., "The History and Literature of 'The New Morality,'" *The Pittsburgh Perspective* 3 (Sept. 1966): 4-17. For an edited version, see *The Situation Debate,* ed. Harvey Cox (Philadelphia: Westminster Press, 1968), pp. 101-16. See also Roger Shinn, "The New Wave in Christian Thought," *Encounter* 28 (Summer 1967): 219-55. For a description of American society at this point in time, see Robert Moskin, "Morality U.S.A.," *Look,* 24 Sept. 1963, pp. 74ff.

2. "Contextual" ethics and "situational" ethics are not synonymous terms, as the subsequent discussion shows. See Paul Lehmann, "Contextual Ethics," in *Dictionary of Christian Ethics,* ed. John Macquarrie (Philadelphia: Westminster Press, 1967), p. 71. See also James F. Childress, "Situation Ethics," in *The Westminster Dictionary of Christian Ethics,* rev. ed., ed. James Childress and John Macquarrie (Philadelphia: Westminster Press, 1986), pp. 586-88.

3. Gustafson, "Context vs. Principles," p. 171.

4. Ibid., p. 173.

Some contextualists have stressed the contextual importance of social relations and structures, others have stressed the self as a center of value, still others have stressed theological perspectives. Clearly each of these contexts affects differently one's interpretation of motives and goals, of values and virtues, of criteria and their application.[5]

Nevertheless, Lehmann does not abandon the term; instead, he gives three reasons why he believes it can be defended. First, the intellectual tradition has always sustained diverse interpretation of terms and methods. Second, Lehmann claims, it *is* possible to give definite meaning to the term. Third, the discipline of ethics needs the challenge that contextualism issues regarding the usefulness of universal and absolute principles and rules.[6]

Lehmann says the debate arose chiefly out of the ethical chaos following World War II.[7] He claims that the historical roots of the debate set contextualism in opposition to both absolutism and relativism:

These circumstances severely challenged the adequacy of traditional ethical standards, on the one hand, and of relativism, on the other. The normative effectiveness of absolutism in ethics seemed more and more impotent and remote. Relativism, as an alternative, tended towards nihilism. The question of a *tertium quid,* a creative option, which might somehow guide ethical sensitivity and responsibility through the impasse posed by absolutism and relativism, seemed long overdue.[8]

5. Lehmann, "Contextual Ethics," p. 72.
6. Ibid. H. Richard Niebuhr's categories (teleological ethics, deontological ethics, and ethics of response), although not escaping the problem of ambiguity altogether, provide more precise descriptions of the different types of ethics than the division between contextual ethics and ethics of principles. See H. Richard Niebuhr, *The Responsible Self: An Essay in Christian Moral Philosophy* (New York: Harper & Row, 1963).
7. Lehmann, "Contextual Ethics," p. 72.
8. Ibid., p. 72.

Lehmann's description makes the continued use of the term "contextualism" compelling. An initial avenue to understanding the term in general lies in examining what those who call themselves contextualists are against. As Lehmann points out, all forms of contextualism stand in opposition to the deductive, casuistic form of ethics that applies absolute principles or laws to each situation. Further, the theologians classified as "contextualists" oppose the entirely antinomian ethic that concentrates its full attention exclusively on the moment of decision. Examples of these two types of ethics will help give a general sense of the parameters of exclusion usually intended by those who identify their ethics as "contextual."

First, contextualism stands against an ethic of universal or absolute law. Of course, as Gustafson points out, there are as many different forms of ethics based on universal principles as there are forms of contextualism. Not only are different principles identified as important for ethical decision, but there is no agreement on what the word "principle" means.[9] These ambiguities notwithstanding, the ethical method identified as "casuistry" provides the best illustration of the deductive approach to ethics that contextualism opposes. Casuistry is a method that provides one with the means to move from the general to the particular in ethical decision-making by applying universal rules and principles to specific cases — thus the designation "deductive."[10]

Although the term "casuistry" can be applied to a variety of ethical traditions, it usually refers to classical Roman Catholic ethics rooted in the Middle Ages. This Catholic system of casuistry was designed to take into account the contingencies of a specific situation that might require exception to a universal rule. In other words, it was an attempt to regulate how and

9. John Bennett, "Principles and the Context," in *Storm over Ethics* (Philadelphia: United Church Press, 1966), pp. 1-25.

10. Geoffrey W. Bromiley, "Casuistry," in *Baker's Dictionary of Christian Ethics,* ed. Carl F. H. Henry (Grand Rapids: Baker Book House, 1973). See also Albert R. Jonsen, "Casuistry," in *The Westminster Dictionary of Christian Ethics,* pp. 78-80.

when one can allow circumstances to modify universal law. As the system developed, casuistry served not only to guide actions in specific situations but also to regulate penitential discipline. The contingencies of the situation were believed to determine the culpability for sin, because the same sin could be deemed more serious in one situation than in another. Thus a complex system arose that determined universal rules of action, exceptions to these rules, degrees of culpability for breaking the rules, and degrees of appropriate punishment. Such codification of these universal laws, exceptions, and penitentials provided detailed rules that attempted to work out in advance what one should do in a particular situation.

While this elaborate system no longer characterizes Roman Catholic moral thought, casuistry as the application of universal rules to particular cases still exists in both Roman Catholic and Protestant ethics. Three primary sources for these universal rules of action exist in Roman Catholic casuistry: biblical texts (particularly commandments), natural moral law, and ecclesiastical tradition. The Protestant tradition has established its own form of casuistical ethics based more exclusively on biblical texts. Divine commandments found in Scripture, particularly the Ten Commandments and the Sermon on the Mount, have been interpreted as eternal divine prescriptions that are valid for all situations.

The primary goal of casuistry is to ascertain God's will in a particular situation, a goal consistent with that of Christian contextualism.[11] The major difference between casuistry and the various forms of contextualism, however, is that the casuist begins with absolute principles and laws and applies them to specific situations, while the contextualist focuses on the specific situation first, believing that moral action cannot be prescribed *in advance* of the actual situation.

While one can clearly identify ethicists who oppose any form of ethics that resorts to absolute laws, the reasons behind this opposition are not uniform; in some cases they are even contradictory. Karl Barth, for instance, is opposed to a deductive ethic

11. Bromiley, "Casuistry," p. 86.

because it *emphasizes* human autonomy and thus rebels against the sovereignty and freedom of divine decision. Joseph Fletcher, on the other hand, is opposed to a deductive ethic because it *denies* human autonomy and does not best serve *agape*.

Despite these differences, however, there are two consistent reasons why contextualists oppose casuistical ethics. First, contextualists charge that the deductive approach cannot take seriously the complexity of ethical decisions. Applying universal laws or principles to a particular situation implies that life is simpler than it really is. A second charge that contextualists often aim at deductive ethics is that it places concern for principles above concern for people and relationships.

The second position opposed by contextualists is one that upholds an antinomian ethic. Because of the contextualists' opposition to absolute laws or principles, they are often charged with advocating an antinomian position. In fact, this has been the most consistent charge against contextualists. This charge, however, contradicts the self-understanding of contextual ethicists, who claim to avoid antinomianism as rigorously as they do the deductive approach to ethics. The best description of an antinomian ethic is found in an essay by the existentialist philosopher Jean-Paul Sartre.

In his essay "Existentialism and Humanism," Sartre rejects universal moral law for two reasons. First, he believes that universal laws are too abstract to be applied successfully to particular situations. Truth and action always require a "concrete environment" that universal laws are incapable of predicting.[12] Second, Sartre's denial of the very existence of universal laws is tied to his denial of the existence of God. He disagrees with philosophers who claim that moral laws are independent of the divine lawgiver. He believes that in denying the existence of God, one realizes that humanity is abandoned, left entirely on its own to establish its own moral values ("Existentialism," p. 34).

---

12. Sartre, "Existentialism and Humanism," in *Existentialism and Humanism* (London: Methuen, 1948), p. 24. All subsequent references to this volume will be made parenthetically in the text.

Sartre's denial of God's existence also leads to the denial of any universal concept of human nature by which human actions can be judged ("Existentialism," p. 28). Each individual has the freedom and the responsibility to create his or her own image of what the self is and what the self ought to do. The primary principle of existentialism, therefore, lies in the idea that "existence precedes essence" — that is, human nature (essence) is defined in the action an individual chooses to take (existence). Through his or her actions an individual seeks not to fulfill some preconceived idea of the "human" but to create such an idea. Therefore, according to Sartre, existentialism "puts every man in possession of himself as he is, and places the entire responsibility for his existence squarely upon his own shoulders" ("Existentialism," p. 29).

Sartre concludes that "every man is condemned to invent man" ("Existentialism," p. 29). In stark contrast to Lehmann, he believes that there are no signs on earth that help define who we are or what we are to do. What the individual takes to be "earthly signs" are actually subject to the individual's own interpretations and choices. By way of example, Sartre tells of a Jesuit priest who interpreted an earlier series of vocational failures as a sign from God that he was not meant to succeed within the secular life but should devote himself to a religious order. While commending the priest's choice, Sartre points out that he could just as easily have interpreted the failures as a sign telling him to become a revolutionary. The interpretation of signs and the choice of action are always left solely to the freedom of individual decision.

Recalling Lehmann's discussion of the fundamental meaning of ethics as outlined in the preceding chapter, it might be argued that Sartre's existentialist ethic includes no concept of security or stability at all. Action appears to be purely random, open to any whim or selfish desire. This is in fact the criticism aimed at all forms of contextual ethics. However, consistent with the fundamental definition of ethics, Sartre claims that existentialism *does* make human life possible ("Existentialism," p. 24). It is not true that existentialism places no restrictions on what is moral. It does not, as its critics often claim, adopt an "anything goes" attitude.[13]

According to Sartre, what makes responsible human action possible is not law or divine activity but a radical sense of human freedom:

> Freedom, in respect of concrete circumstances, can have no other end and aim but itself; and when once a man has seen that values depend upon himself, in that state of forsakenness he can will only one thing, and that is freedom as the foundation of all values. . . . The actions of men of good faith have, as their ultimate significance, the quest of freedom itself as such. ("Existentialism," p. 19)

Responsible action results from the recognition that freedom is the basic condition of being human. Initially, one speaks of this freedom from the perspective of the individual. But freedom never involves the individual alone. While we "will freedom for freedom's sake . . . in and through particular circumstances," Sartre claims that what we discover is that our freedom "depends entirely upon the freedom of others and that the freedom of others depends upon our own" ("Existentialism," pp. 51-52).[14] There is a necessary reciprocity here that makes concern for individual freedom inextricably connected to concern for the freedom of all.

13. Sartre believes that the existentialist ethic is a form of humanism because it reminds humanity that there is no lawgiver but humanity itself. However, he sets existential humanism against any claim that humanity is an "end-in-self" or "the supreme value," claiming that such a "cult of humanity ends in Comtian humanism, shut-in upon itself, and — this must be said — in Fascism. We do not want a humanism like that" (ibid., p. 55).

14. Carl Michalson describes this aspect of Sartre's existentialist ethic by claiming that "the norm" used by Sartre to determine what one must do in a given situation is that "one must so act as to let others be free while oneself remain[s] free." Michalson claims that it is a mistake to argue that an existentialist ethic is interested only in the individual (Michalson, "Existentialist Ethics," in *The Westminster Dictionary of Christian Ethics*, p. 218).

Critics who charge that existentialism isolates the individual and rejects the solidarity of humankind are, according to Sartre, misdirected. Although the individual alone must choose the course of action he or she takes, that choice in itself creates an image of what the individual believes all persons should be and do. In choosing a course of action, the individual makes a decision for that which he or she believes is valuable — that is, chooses "the better" over "the worse," but, as Sartre explains, "nothing can be better for us unless it is better for all" ("Existentialism," p. 29). Each person, therefore, is responsible not only for his or her own actions but also for the meaning of those actions for all humankind. The individual creates an image of what is human whenever he or she acts. "I am thus responsible for myself and for all men," Sartre says, "and I am creating a certain image of man as I would have him to be. In fashioning myself I fashion man" ("Existentialism," p. 30).

Sartre demonstrates his understanding of this radical freedom in light of the uselessness of universal law by presenting the dilemma of a student who came to him for advice during World War II. The student faced the choice of staying at home to care for his mother or joining the resistance movement. If he stayed with his mother, he knew he would aid one particular individual. If he joined the French Free Forces, he might possibly help a greater number of people, but there was no guarantee that he would. Which ethical system could give him an answer to his dilemma? In this case the Christian maxim to love one's neighbor did not tell him who his neighbor was. The Kantian ethic requiring that one never treat another as a means did not tell him what to do when either choice of action required treating one person or group (his mother or the soldiers) as a means for the sake of the other. How was he to decide between two good actions, each of which canceled out the other?

Sartre's response to the student illustrates his emphasis on freedom: "You are free, therefore choose — that is to say, invent. No rule of general morality can show you what you ought to do: no signs are vouchsafed in this world" ("Existentialism," p. 38). Sartre went on to make this assertion:

By what authority, in the name of what golden rule of morality do you think he could have decided in perfect peace of mind, either to abandon his mother or to remain with her? There are no means of judging. The content is always concrete, and therefore unpredictable; it has always to be invented. The one thing that counts, is to know whether the invention is made in the name of freedom. ("Existentialism," pp. 52-53)

In short, each individual is entirely responsible for his or her actions. No general concept of human nature and no universal rules or principles can define the self. Self-definition comes solely through an act of the will. "We are what we do" in each specific situation.

Sartre's extreme form of antinomianism is often used as a charge against all ethicists who foreswear universal principles and emphasize the situation in which one makes moral decisions. The tendency to group all such ethicists together leads to a caricature of the contextual quality of various approaches to ethics. One can legitimately appreciate or abhor Sartre's radical emphases on human freedom and on the moment of decision-making; one cannot legitimately claim that all ethics which have a contextual character are synonymous with atheistic existentialism.[15]

So far in this project, "contextualism" has been used in the most general sense to refer to any ethic that foreswears the application of universal principles and rules to particular situations and instead emphasizes the particular situation of decision-making. The word, however, needs more precise definition. It cannot, for instance, refer to the antinomian approach of existentialism that we see in Sartre's work, for Chris-

---

15. This radically antinomian and relativistic position of existentialism drew the Catholic Church into the debate over context versus principles. A few Catholic scholars, notably in France, defended the less extreme forms of Christian existentialist ethics, believing they provided a needed criticism of the abuses of traditional Catholic ethics. See John C. Ford, S.J., and Gerald Kelly, S.J., *Contemporary Moral Theology*, Volume I: *Questions in Fundamental Moral Theology* (Westminster: Newman Press, 1969), chs. 5-7.

tian contextualists foreswear this more antinomian vision of ethics. It is also important to develop a more precise definition in order to distinguish between the situation ethics of Joseph Fletcher and the contextual ethics of Lehmann and others. In the following sections I will explore how the ethics of Joseph Fletcher, Karl Barth, and Stanley Hauerwas compare with the ethics of Paul Lehmann. One conclusion of this discussion will be that while the theological ethics of Barth, Hauerwas, and Lehmann can be called "Christian contextualism," Fletcher's ethics, when examined closely, belongs to another category.

Situation Ethics: Joseph Fletcher

In his book entitled *Situation Ethics: The New Morality,* Joseph Fletcher identifies love as the only absolute in Christian ethics.[16] Love alone, he says, is intrinsically good. It is the only rule or principle that is never altered, that both guides action and evaluates the consequences of action.[17] Like other ethicists who are called "contextual," Fletcher opposes what he understands as two distortions of Christian ethics: legalism and antinomianism.

Regarding the former, Fletcher is, as Gustafson says,

16. Fletcher, *Situation Ethics: The New Morality* (Philadelphia: Westminster Press, 1966). All subsequent references to this volume will be made parenthetically in the text. See also these works: "The New Look in Christian Ethics," *Harvard Divinity Bulletin* 24, no. 1, pp. 7-18; "Contemporary Conscience: A Christian Method," *Kenyon Alumni Bulletin* 21, no. 3 (July-Sept. 1963): 4-10; "Love Is the Only Measure," *Commonweal,* 14 Jan. 1966, pp. 427-32; "What's in a Rule?: A Situationist's View," in *Norm and Context in Christian Ethics,* ed. Gene H. Outka and Paul Ramsey (New York: Charles Scribner's Sons, 1968), pp. 325-49; "Reflection and Reply," *The Situation Ethics Debate,* ed. Harvey Cox (Philadelphia: Westminster Press, 1968), pp. 249-64.

17. According to Fletcher, situation ethics borrows two guidelines from Saint Paul: "The written code kills, but the Spirit gives life" (2 Cor. 3:6), and "For the whole law is fulfilled in one word, 'You shall love your neighbor as yourself'" (Gal. 5:14). See Fletcher, *Situation Ethics,* p. 30.

"passionate in his distress at any sign of legalism."[18] He vehemently attacks the legalistic tendencies of Orthodox Judaism, Catholicism, and Protestantism. Believing that universal law cannot adequately anticipate what one should do in a concrete situation, he claims that the legalism of these traditions ignores the complexities of human life. Each tradition's attempt to provide exceptions to the rules for particular circumstances uncovers the inability of universal law to anticipate adequately what one should do in a concrete situation. Fletcher also believes that such legalism lacks compassion, because it elevates adherence to the law above concern for human beings.

However, Fletcher is as eager to distance himself from antinomianism (represented, he says, by "the Gnostics") as he is to distance himself from legalism:

> While legalists are preoccupied with law and its stipulations, the Gnostics are so flatly opposed to law — even in principle — that their moral decisions are random, unpredictable, erratic. . . . They are not only "unbound by the chain of law" but actually sheer extemporizers, impromptu and intellectually irresponsible. They not only cast the old Torah aside; they even cease to think seriously and carefully about the demands of love as it has been shown in Christ, the love norm itself. The baby goes out with the bath water! (*Situation Ethics,* p. 23)

Fletcher equates this position with the ethics of existentialism.

He seeks to avoid the random particularity of existentialism by claiming that love provides the only absolute norm for ethics. In contrast to legalism, the demands of love allow all other principles and laws to be suspended. Fletcher believes that his commitment "to persons rather than principles" prevents him from falling into the errors of legalism; his reliance on *agape* as the only absolute norm keeps him from falling into the errors of antinomianism. The next question, however, is this: How do we know what the demands of love are?

18. Gustafson, "How Does Love Reign?" *Christian Century,* 18 May 1966, p. 654.

In the answer to this question we find the real key to Fletcher's ethics and that which clearly distinguishes his work from that of Paul Lehmann. Love, according to Fletcher, must form a coalition with utilitarianism. Situation ethics "takes over from Bentham and Mill the strategic principle of 'the greatest good of the greatest number,'" although in doing so it "reshapes the 'good' of the utilitarians, replacing their pleasure principle with *agape*" (*Situation Ethics,* p. 95).

Fletcher's emphasis on utilitarianism leads him to discard the concept of "necessary evil" — that is, the acknowledgment that an action can be necessary and yet not good. Fletcher does not readily recognize tragic situations in which one is faced with only evil choices. Rather, he claims that all actions that are done out of a love which calculates how to serve the greatest number of people are good. Thus, for example, if a lie serves a loving purpose, the lie is not a necessary evil but a positive good, and no forgiveness for telling the lie is necessary. "If love vetoes the truth, so be it," asserts Fletcher. "The situationist holds that whatever is the most loving thing in the situation is the right and good thing. It is not excusably evil, it is positively good" (*Situation Ethics,* p. 65).

Fletcher's interpretation of *agape* leads him to make six propositions for ethics. First, he claims that "only one thing is intrinsically good, namely love." The value of everything else is determined only in relation to concrete circumstances; only *agape* has value in itself. Second, he says that "the ruling norm of Christian decision is love, nothing else." Third, Fletcher believes that "love and justice are the same, for justice is love distributed, nothing else." Fourth, seeking to avoid a sentimental understanding of Christian love, Fletcher claims that "love wills the neighbor's good, whether we like him or not." In the fifth proposition, Fletcher emphasizes his utilitarian approach when he states that "only the end justifies the means, nothing else." Finally, he claims that "love's decisions are made situationally, not prescriptively."[19]

19. Each of these propositions constitutes the title of a chapter in Fletcher's book.

47

Regarding this last proposition, Fletcher criticizes Lehmann for bringing ambiguity to the term "contextualism" by giving it two meanings. He claims that by "contextualism" Lehmann sometimes means that Christian action is carried out in the context of faith within the *koinonia,* but at other times means that "Christian action should be tailored to fit objective circumstances" (*Situation Ethics,* p. 14). Fletcher explains that he uses the term in the second sense, believing that the first is redundant: all Christian ethics, he says, are done in the context of faith. The consistent question posed to Fletcher by his critics, however, is whether Fletcher's own method of ethics reflects the context of faith.

It is extremely difficult to identify what difference the "context of faith" makes to Fletcher's method, since reference to Christ is not a component essential to it. Christology enters his argument only in the book's appendix. The principle of utilitarianism, not articles of faith, governs Fletcher's ethic. Fletcher himself admits that "except for a stress on the normative ideal of 'love,' which is always carefully defined as New Testament *agape,*" he makes very little reference to any "theological framework" (*Situation Ethics,* p. 15). Situation ethics, he says, "is not particularly Catholic or Protestant or Orthodox or humanist. It extricates us from the *odium theologicum*" (*Situation Ethics,* p. 13). Although Fletcher claims that we must ask "What has God done?" in making Christian ethical decisions, in the final analysis that doesn't really seem to matter. In Fletcher's method *agape* is finally an independent concept divorced from incarnational theology (*Situation Ethics,* p. 152).

The works of Paul Lehmann and Joseph Fletcher have often been identified as positing similar approaches to ethics. It has often been assumed that Lehmann's "contextual" ethic and Fletcher's "situational" ethic represent the same method. This is true only in the most general sense, in that each of them foreswears universal laws and emphasizes the context of decision-making. Indeed, their ethics are so different that one might agree with Gustafson when he says that a comparison of them disproves the usefulness of the category "contextualism." The fact of the matter is that Fletcher's ethic needs to be classified under a different rubric.

As pointed out earlier in Chapter One, H. Richard Niebuhr identifies not two but three approaches to ethics. Fletcher obviously rejects the option of an ethic of law. However, his work, unlike Lehmann's, cannot be placed in Niebuhr's category of an ethic of response. Given his alliance with utilitarianism, Fletcher himself has described his method as coming "closer to teleology" than to Niebuhr's ethic of response (*Situation Ethics,* p. 96).[20]

Lehmann has registered his disagreement with Fletcher's approach to ethics.[21] Unlike Fletcher, he does not identify *agape* as the one absolute of Christian ethics; what some call "love monism" is not characteristic of his work. If Lehmann emphasizes any one concept more than another, it is the concept of "humanization." He does not, however, intend for his interpretation of "that which makes and keeps human life human" to become an absolute norm of Christian ethics in the same way in which Fletcher proposes that *agape* become a norm.

Lehmann is in fact highly critical of Fletcher's approach to ethics because of Fletcher's failure to demonstrate that Christology is a necessary ingredient for Christian ethics. While the Incarnation is almost absent in Fletcher's utilitarianism, it stands at the heart of Lehmann's "contextualism." Lehmann also objects to Fletcher's calculated approach to ethics, which he believes can become as rigid as the legalism that Fletcher opposes.[22]

20. See also "What's in a Rule?" p. 342.

21. Lehmann expressed his opinion in a book review of *Situation Ethics.* The review was published in the September 1966 issue of the *Episcopal Theological School Bulletin.* A shorter version was published in *The Situation Ethics Debate,* edited by Harvey Cox.

22. This surprising rigidity can be noted in Fletcher's account of a case involving the question of abortion. A young woman was raped by a fellow patient in a mental hospital. Based on the principle that taking a human life is immoral, the hospital refused to honor the request made by the girl's father that the pregnancy be terminated. In contrast, Fletcher describes the contextualists' position:

> They would in all likelihood favor abortion for the sake of the patient's physical and mental health, not only if it were needed to save her life. It

Lehmann criticizes Fletcher by raising a pointed question: "If 'what is precisely and exactly and starkly unique about the Christian ethic is Christ' how can an Appendix express this difference other than as co-incidentally, inferentially, and vaguely?" Lehmann is particularly critical of Fletcher's willingness to interchange the statements "Situation ethics is Christian ethics" and "Christian ethics is situation ethics." To him such an interchange shows that Fletcher has exchanged the uniqueness of Christ in Christian decision-making for "a simplistic love reductionism."[23]

Lehmann believes that the connecting factor which binds individual ethical decisions together is the story of God's gracious movement in Jesus Christ on behalf of creation. This story sets the parameters for human existence and behavior. Fletcher, on the other hand, believes that the parameters are set by the utilitarian use of the principle of *agape*.[24] Christian faith may

---

is even likely they would favor abortion for the sake of the victim's self-respect or reputation or happiness or simply on the ground that no unwanted and unintended baby should ever be born. (Fletcher, *Situation Ethics*, p. 39)

In claiming that the contextualists could argue for abortion "simply on the ground that no unwanted and unintended baby should ever be born," Fletcher seems to provide us with a universal rule, thereby contradicting his own claims against absolute negatives and absolute affirmatives.

23. Lehmann believes that Fletcher's reductionism leads him into the same errors as those of the groups he argues against (pietists, moralists, legalists, and antinomians), and puts him at odds with the movements he advocates: pragmatism, relativism, positivism, and personalism. "For these movements, Christ was indeed superfluous, and love a normative value arrived at by reason, and functioning by the utilitarian rule of reason which Fletcher, like Paul Ramsey, also adopts. In the case of Fletcher's abhorrents, Christ was 'de-situationalized' by disconnection; in the case of Fletcher's adoptions, Christ was 'ex-institutionalized' by being ignored. Fletcher tries to avoid both distortions by substituting one of his own. In this account of situation ethics, Christ is made to fit into the vestigial mold of an 'Appendix'" ("The Decalogue and a Human Future," original manuscript, p. 5).

24. Even when Fletcher allows room for regret over a necessary action, he will not allow for guilt or remorse. His utilitarian principles, it seems, make it simple to have an easy conscience. This becomes clearer when one compares Fletcher's views of the concept of "necessary evil" with those of Alexander Miller. After interviewing a group of French resistance fighters

add the motivation for action in the Christian community. It does not, however, change the content.

An Ethic Based on the
Specific Command of God: Karl Barth

The roots of the debate over context versus principles extend to the writings of European theologians who have sought to work out the ethical implications of Reformed theology's emphasis on justification by faith.[25] Seminal works in this vein include Karl Barth's *Church Dogmatics*, Emil Brunner's *The Divine Imperative,* and Dietrich Bonhoeffer's *Ethics.*[26] Edward Long points out that the terms "contextualism," "situation ethics," and "the new morality" were not used to describe the content of these works at the time of their publication. Nevertheless, because they challenge prescriptive forms of ethics and have greatly influenced subsequent scholars who have proposed contextualism as an ethical method, these works are part of the debate. Among Barth, Brunner, and Bonhoeffer, Barth is the one whose work stands closest to that of Lehmann. An examination of *Church Dogmatics* proves the point.

---

in World War II who had to steal, lie, and kill in order to survive, Miller asserted, "If killing and lying are to be used, it must be under the most urgent pressure of social necessity, and with a profound sense of guilt that no better way can be presently found." Fletcher disagrees, claiming, "We should change [Miller's] 'guilt' to sorrow, since such tragic situations are a cause for regret, but not for remorse" (*Situation Ethics*, p. 124). The consequence of disregarding the concept of "necessary evil" is that Fletcher does not live up to his own insistence that the complexities of a given life-situation be taken seriously. His method of combining love with utilitarianism appears to render ethical decision-making a simplistic task. Because he believes that "love could justify anything," divine forgiveness is not needed even in the most tragic human choices. This seems to be a strange contradiction in an ethics that is based on New Testament *agape*.

25. Long, "The History and Literature of 'The New Morality,'" p. 104.

26. All three of these theologians have had substantial influence on the work of Paul Lehmann. Only Karl Barth will be discussed in this chapter.

According to Barth, the task of theological ethics is "to understand the Word of God as the command of God."[27] Therefore, ethics forms a part of the doctrine of God and cannot be separated from dogmatics.

Consistent with his presentation of other doctrines, Barth's doctrine of the "command of God" does not begin with Christian anthropology (in this case with human action) but with the action of God or with what he calls "divine ethics." Accordingly, theological ethics does not ask "What is the Good?" and "How are we to achieve it?" (II/2: 518). Rather, it knows that the answers to these questions are already given in God's grace (II/2: 519). It is the divine action in Jesus Christ that determines what is good human action and constitutes the starting point of theological ethics (II/2: 538).[28] In his discussion, however, Barth does not simply focus on divine action. The divine command, he points out, always has a corresponding conception of human responsibility. In answering the question "What are we to do?" Barth describes human action as "correspondence" to divine action — that is, human action is to "render an account of God's grace."

Barth's approach to ethics opposes both casuistry and antinomianism. He defines casuistry as that system of ethics which interprets divine commands found in biblical texts, natural law, and ecclesiastical tradition as legal claims that must be applied to each specific situation (III/4: 6). Barth says it is tempting to

27. Barth, *Church Dogmatics,* 4 vols., ed. Thomas F. Torrance, trans. Geoffrey W. Bromiley (Edinburgh: T. & T. Clark, 1936-1969), III/4: 4 (all subsequent references to this volume will be made parenthetically in the text). Barth's first developed treatment of ethics in *Church Dogmatics* falls at the end of his volume on the doctrine of God (II/2). He intended three more sections on ethics to follow: "The Command of God the Creator," "The Command of God the Reconciler," and "The Command of God the Redeemer." But he completed only the section on the ethics of creation (III/4). He died before completing his draft on the ethics of reconciliation and never began writing about the ethics of redemption. The collection of the ethical writings Barth completed prior to the *Dogmatics* is entitled *Ethics,* ed. Dietrich Braun (New York: Seabury Press, 1981).

28. Lehmann, of course, agrees completely with Barth that only from the humanity of Jesus Christ do we know who we are and what we are to do.

accept casuistry as the best route for Christian ethics, because it so clearly defines good and evil without tyrannizing the conscience. Nevertheless, he rejects casuistry for three reasons.

First, he claims that casuistry's assumption that the moralist can judge precisely between good and evil leads to idolatry by setting the moral agent on a plane with God (III/4: 10). In interpreting the law as the sole will of God and believing that one can master the law, casuistry suggests that one can master God. At best, casuistry's interpretation of "divine command and human application" allows for a co-determination between God and humanity of what action is to be taken, God providing the general rule and humanity providing the content of specific action (II/2: 664ff.).

Second, in claiming that God's will is a universal rule which can be applied to each situation, casuistry interprets God's command as an "empty form" that requires human application to a specific situation to provide its content. In contrast, Barth claims that while the command of God is given "universally and formally," it is always also "an individual command for the conduct of this man, at this moment and in this situation" (III/4: 11).

Third, Barth argues that casuistry destroys Christian freedom (III/4: 13). By "freedom" Barth does not mean "freedom of choice" whereby one is given God's command and then can choose to obey or not. Rather, he means the freedom to obey God — that is, the freedom to orient one's whole being to God's command at each moment. The freedom to choose to follow a command or not implies that human obedience has to do only with specific acts in relation to a specific law. Barth argues that obedience to God involves the whole person. Casuistry "encroaches too little" upon humanity because it does not demand enough (III/4: 14).

Having rejected casuistry, Barth also rejects what he calls "piecemeal" (antinomian) ethics — ethics that claim we should be "governed from moment to moment and situation to situation by a kind of direct and particular divine inspiration and guidance" (III/4: 15). Barth claims that the radical particularity of God's command implies that an individual has no other recourse in decision-making than to listen to the command of the hour, to await the inspiration of the Holy Spirit who speaks to each given situation. According to this interpretation, God can command one course of action in one situation and give an entirely contradictory command in another. The individual can neither explain the particular course of action taken nor persuade others to similar action on any other basis than an appeal to having heard the Word of God at the moment of decision.

It is important to note that Barth agrees with piecemeal ethics in some limited ways. A Christian ethic, he says, is *at least* this, because it preserves the idea of the freedom of God (III/4: 16). According to Barth, God "never simply repeats Himself. . . . His mercy is new every morning and therefore new for every man and for him in every situation" (III/4: 16). Furthermore, piecemeal ethics preserves the particularity of divine action. Theological ethics is not interested in hypothetical situations, humanity in general, or general concepts of human action. It is concerned with what "we ourselves ought to do in our given situation." It is in each given moment of moral decision that God's command is revealed and obeyed: "The divine command is the particular command which faces each of our decisions, the specially relevant individual command for the decision which we have to make at this moment and in this situation" (II/2: 654, 662).

Nevertheless, Barth disagrees with the suggestion of piecemeal ethics that God's command comes as a series of unrelated events with no continuity between one command and another. There are no "absolutely individual cases," he insists (III/4: 17). According to Barth, ethics has nothing to do with casuistry, but neither is it exhausted in reference to the specific situation (III/4: 17).

Divine commands are not broken into atomized, separate, and unrelated events in the life of the individual or the community. Rather, the individual commands of God are all set within the broader context of God's history with humanity. This history is the "story of God's grace," which includes creation, reconciliation, and redemption. This story of God's action in relation to human action is the "constant factor" needed to provide the connection between various ethical decisions (III/4: 26). The obedience of the individual to each particular command in any given situation is to give witness to the broader context of God's history of grace with humanity: "God wills this and that particular thing because He wills the actualization of this election of Grace . . . and therefore prepares us for the office of witness" (II/2: 678).

Barth's concept of witness provides a reinterpretation of the *imitatio Christi*. Christian moral action does not follow a direct, literal imitation of the deeds of Jesus, for this would lead to a claim of equality with Christ; we would believe that we, like Christ, could become "gracious Lords" to our neighbor. Such a view underestimates the pervasiveness of human sin and is itself a form of sin in that humanity attempts to be like God. Correspondence with God's gracious action in Christ, however, neither requires nor allows human action to seek such equality: "Neither for ourselves nor for others can we do the good which God does for us" (II/2: 578). Human action is not a literal imitation of God's grace but renders an account of this grace (II/2: 576). Just as the parables of Jesus provide pictures of the kingdom of God, so human action is to present an image of God's grace.

Barth identifies the contextual nature of ethics in two ways. He refers to the specific situation in which God commands individuals or groups to particular action, and he also refers to the story of God's grace as providing the context for divine command and human responsibility.

Lehmann's work shares many similarities with that of Barth. In fact, he may indeed be the "American Barth," as some have suggested, in that he builds on many of the foundations laid by the Swiss scholar. Even so, Lehmann does not simply repeat what Barth has already said, and in certain ways they have different views. One significant difference between them lies in Barth's emphasis on divine command. Lehmann agrees with Barth's decision to place ethics in the context of divine election, but he believes that Barth's early work allowed the divine imperative to overshadow the divine indicative — that is, allowed

God's commands to overshadow God's action as God relates to the world.[29] Although Lehmann does not think that the command of God should be excluded from ethics, he does not want to give it a primary place.

As late as 1960, H. Richard Niebuhr still claimed that Barth's ethic emphasized divine command. Accordingly, he placed Barth's ethic in the category of "deontological ethics" — that is, categorized it as an ethic of law. Niebuhr's assessment notwithstanding, a strong argument can be made for placing Barth's ethic in the category of an ethic of response. Although Barth's continued emphasis on divine command even in his later work distinguishes his ethic somewhat from that of both Lehmann and Niebuhr, his interpretation of command as "permission" makes the distinction less acute.

An Ethic of Character: Stanley Hauerwas

Stanley Hauerwas also stands among those theologians who foreswear an ethic of absolutes and a thoroughly antinomian ethic.[30]

29. Lehmann, "The Foundation and Pattern of Christian Behavior," in *Christian Faith and Social Action: Essays in Honor of Reinhold Niebuhr,* ed. John A. Hutchison (New York: Charles Scribner's Sons, 1953), pp. 100-101. See also Niebuhr, *The Responsible Self,* 66 and 131.

30. Hauerwas has chosen to write primarily through the essay. His books of collected essays include the following: *Vision and Virtue: Essays in Ethical Reflection* (Notre Dame: University of Notre Dame Press, 1974); *Truthfulness and Tragedy: Further Investigation into Christian Ethics,* co-authored with Richard Bondi and David B. Burrell (Notre Dame: University of Notre Dame Press, 1977); *A Community of Character: Toward a Constructive Christian Social Ethic* (Notre Dame: University of Notre Dame Press, 1981); *Suffering Presence: Theological Reflections on Medicine, the Mentally Handicapped, and the Church* (Notre Dame: University of Notre Dame Press, 1986).

His other books include *Character and the Christian Life: A Study in Theological Ethics* (San Antonio: Trinity University Press, 1975); *The Peaceable Kingdom: A Primer in Christian Ethics* (Notre Dame: University of Notre Dame Press, 1983); *Resident Aliens: Life in the Christian Colony,* co-authored with William H. Willimon (Nashville: Abingdon Press, 1989); *Why Narrative? Readings in Narrative Theology,* co-edited with L. Gregory Jones

In the first instance, he believes that the search for absolutes is both futile and dangerous — futile because there is no way to establish the absolute character of principles, and dangerous because claims for absolute truth lead communities to force their truth on others. The quest for absolutes, he says, "only makes us more susceptible to violence."[31] In the second instance, Hauerwas opposes a "piecemeal" or antinomian approach to ethics through his objection to reducing ethics to "hard cases." Such a reduction, he claims, neglects the need for us to develop identities that enable us to make those hard decisions (*Peaceable Kingdom*, p. 3). Ethics has to do not only with specific moments of decision-making but also with building the character and identity of the moral agent prior to the making of moral decisions.

Hauerwas's rejection of absolute moral rules and ethical occasionalism stems from his understanding of the function of theology and ethics and of the relationship between the two. Christian ethics, he claims, *is* theology — that is, theology and ethics are part and parcel of the same discipline. One does not first set out to outline a systematic theology and then discuss its ethical implications (*Peaceable Kingdom*, p. xvii). Rather, theology is ethics from the very beginning. Theology is not constituted solely by reflection on Christian doctrine and beliefs, Hauerwas claims: "Christian convictions are by nature meant to form and illumine lives" (*Peaceable Kingdom*, p. xviii). Ethics, on the other hand, does not focus solely on a series of moral decisions. Rather, as a theological endeavor, ethics seeks to give shape to Christian character and vision. Christian theology and ethics, therefore, share the common task of giving Christians a sense of who they are and what they are to do. Out of this understanding, three characteristics of Hauerwas's ethic become important: character, vision, and narrative.

(Grand Rapids: Eerdmans, 1989); and *Naming the Silences: God, Medicine, and the Problem of Suffering* (Grand Rapids: Eerdmans, 1990).

31. Hauerwas, *The Peaceable Kingdom*, p. 6. All subsequent references to this volume will be made parenthetically in the text.

Character. Hauerwas says that ethics concentrates not on good deeds but on good persons. Much like Lehmann, Hauerwas sees ethics as providing the ethos in which responsible human beings are formed. This ethos contributes to the character formation of Christians in the context of Christian community. Here Hauerwas's concept of character formation runs parallel in many respects to Lehmann's concept of maturity. Like Lehmann, Hauerwas has an interest in the formation of Christian identity that leads him to emphasize the church as the primary locus of Christian ethics. The task of Christian ethics, according to Hauerwas, is to examine the extent to which Christian action conforms to the vision and mission of the Christian church.

Vision. According to Hauerwas, Christian ethics "is not first of all concerned with 'thou shalt' or 'thou shalt not.' Its first task is to help us rightly envision the world" (*Peaceable Kingdom,* p. 29). Referring to Iris Murdoch's concept, Hauerwas says that people's total vision of life is demonstrated "in their mode of speech or silence, their choices of words, their assessments of others, their conceptions of their own lives, what they think attractive or praiseworthy . . . in short, the configurations of their thought which show continually in their reactions and conversations."[32] Hauerwas believes that our moral assessment of people does not simply focus on the particular decisions people make but also includes their vision of life. Ethics has to do not only with rational argument but also with the vision we have of the world.[33]

Christian doctrines, therefore, describe not only what Christians believe but also the vision Christians have of the world and of their place in it. Hauerwas emphasizes this vision when he, like Lehmann, summarizes the three affirmations of Christian anthropology — that is, human beings are creatures, sinners, and believers (*Peaceable Kingdom,* p. 28). In affirming that they are creatures, Christians recognize that life is a gift from God. Christians acknowledge the existence of sin when they

32. Hauerwas, *Vision and Virtue,* p. 35.
33. Ibid.

recognize the fundamental rebellion in the world against this gift of life that God has given. And Christians acknowledge their redemption when they see themselves as God's people living in the context of God's history.[34] In approaching specific moral dilemmas such as abortion or war, Christians embracing this vision do not simply turn to a prescribed set of rules or principles to make their decision but act in ways consistent with their vision of the world described by these doctrines. However, doctrines are not the primary source of the Christian vision; they simply reflect and describe a vision that is already there. The primary source of the vision of the Christian community is the narrative out of which it lives.

Narrative. According to Hauerwas, our present tendency to reduce ethics to reflection on "moral quandaries" demonstrates that we are a people without a history (*Peaceable Kingdom*, p. 116). The same can be said for our tendency to look for a universal ethic unqualified by who we are as a people. Hauerwas asserts that the very quandaries we confront and how we confront them "depend on the kind of people we are and the way we have learned to construe the world through our language, habits and feelings" (*Peaceable Kingdom*, p. 117). The primary moral question, therefore, is not what one ought to do but who one ought to be. We learn who we are from the narrative that forms our life, not from a basic set of convictions that distinguishes right from wrong behavior (*Peaceable Kingdom*, p. 118).[35] Thus, according to Hauerwas, "the nature of Christian ethics is determined by the fact that Christian convictions take the form of a story, or perhaps better, a set of stories that constitutes a tradition, which in turn creates and forms a community. Christian ethics does not begin by emphasizing rules or principles, but by calling our attention to a narrative that tells of God's dealing with creation" (*Peaceable Kingdom*, pp. 24-25).

34. It should be noted that Hauerwas does not establish this Christian anthropology as the foundation of his ethics. The primary doctrine of Christian ethics is election.

35. For further comment on Hauerwas's understanding of narrative, see Chapter Three.

Hauerwas's ethics and Lehmann's ethics are probably closer in method than the ethics of any other two contemporary theologians. A major difference, however, lies in Hauerwas's position as a pacifist. Hauerwas stresses the "centrality of nonviolence as the hallmark of the Christian moral life." Such a stance, he says, "is not just an option for a few, but [is] incumbent on all Christians who seek to live faithfully in the kingdom made possible by the life, death, and resurrection of Jesus. Nonviolence is not one among other behavioral implications that can be drawn from the gospel but is integral to the shape of Christian convictions" (*Peaceable Kingdom,* p. xvi). While Lehmann agrees that the Gospel is committed to nonviolence, his ethic makes room for necessary evil at certain junctures in a fashion that Hauerwas will not allow.

A Contextual Ethic: Paul Lehmann

Contextualism,[36] Lehmann tells us, is a method for systematic theology that seeks to relate the content of theology (the self-

36. Lehmann's article entitled "The Foundation and Pattern of Christian Behavior," published in 1953, helped initiate the American debate in theological ethics over context vs. principles. Throughout the 1950s, a number of works by American theologians set forth, like Lehmann's work, the implications of Reformed theology for contemporary Christian ethics and were classified as works on "contextual ethics." They included Joseph Sittler's *Structure of Christian Ethics* (Baton Rouge: Louisiana State University Press, 1958); Alexander Miller's *Renewal of Man: A Twentieth-Century Essay on Justification by Faith* (Garden City, N.Y.: Doubleday, 1955); Albert T. Rasmussen's *Christian Social Ethics: Exerting Christian Influence* (Englewood Cliffs, N.J.: Prentice-Hall, 1956); and James Gustafson's article entitled "Christian Faith and Social Action," in *Faith and Ethics: The Theology of H. Richard Niebuhr,* ed. Paul Ramsey (New York: Harper & Brothers, 1957). In 1963, a decade after his initiating article, Lehmann offered further development of his ideas about contextualism in his book entitled *Ethics in a Christian Context.* In that same year *The Responsible Self* by H. Richard Niebuhr was posthumously published. Niebuhr's exposition of relational ethics provides a clear ethical category that encompasses most aspects of contextual ethics.

disclosing activity of God in Jesus Christ) to the setting of theology (the concrete situation out of which theology as a discipline arises).[37] Lehmann fears that if one overemphasizes either the content or the setting, one risks making theology irrelevant, for both errors abstract the Christian faith from everyday living. By overemphasizing the content, one risks stressing the transcendence of God to the point of removing God from human history altogether. By overemphasizing the setting, one makes God expendable — that is, one methodologically removes God from consideration.

Lehmann's contextual method seeks to avoid irrelevance by emphasizing the relationship between God's incarnational activity and human response to this activity, an emphasis bequeathed to us by Reformed theology:

> As the Reformers saw it, revelation and faith came to life in the reality of a dynamic interrelation between the initiative of God and the concrete acts of men in response to this initiative. These two kinds of acts could be neither identified nor isolated the one from the other. They belonged dialectically together. . . . In a similar way, a contextual theology tries to express the dynamics of divine initiative and human response through a dialectic of analysis and criticism which interrelates the referential [content] and the phenomenological factors [setting] in the doing of theology.[38]

According to Lehmann, the contextual character of Christian ethics grows out of the very nature of divine activity. He argues, therefore, that the proper question of the debate regarding contextualism lies not in the general issues of "prescription vs. freedom" or "law vs. love" but in this *theological* question: What

37. "A contextual method for systematic theology," Lehmann says, "concentrates attention upon the dynamic and dialectical relation between the phenomenological and the referential aspects of the theological task" (Lehmann, "On Doing Theology: A Contextual Possibility," in *Prospect for Theology: Essays in Honour of H. H. Farmer,* ed. F. G. Healey [Welwyn Garden City, Eng.: James Nisbet & Co., 1966], p. 132).

38. Lehmann, "On Doing Theology," p. 133.

difference does the life, death, and resurrection of Christ make for responsible human behavior?[39]

Lehmann does not, of course, suggest that the debate has nothing to do with the distinction between rules and context. The Christological focus of ethics, however, means that the debate over the contextual character of Christian ethics cannot revolve around a meta-ethical question which can be debated with or without reference to Christ. For *Christian* ethics the debate focuses on the significance of Christ for human action. The difference between rules and context is examined, but only within the larger context of the Incarnation:

> It does make a very real difference to the moral significance of the actions and decisions of men whether priority in judging and guiding these actions and decisions is given to law or to love, to Moses or to Jesus, to "the letter which killeth" or to "the spirit which giveth life," as Jesus himself once put it. The difference is that between a morality which steadily loses effective contact both with its creative setting and with its concrete relation to behavior, and a morality which steadily draws upon its creative setting for the perspective and the power to shape the motives and patterns, the decisions and actions of behavior.[40]

According to Lehmann, the Incarnation sets Christian ethics on the contextualist path by teaching us that God's action is "concrete," "integrative," and "free."

First, incarnational theology understands that God's activity is concrete. Divine activity always occurs in the context of human history. One of Lehmann's reactions against an absolutist ethic is that it applies exterior principles to the situation. God's activity, on the other hand, occurs within the context of human events and therefore requires not human *application* but human *discernment*. Thus Lehmann speaks of God's activity discerned in "signs" and events of this world.

39. Lehmann, "The New Morality: A Sermon for Lent," *Dialogue* 5 (Winter 1966): 53.

40. Ibid., p. 54.

Because divine activity is concrete, occurring in the real world, Christian behavior cannot be characterized by retreat. Because God's actions are discerned only in concrete historical events, Christians must notice what is happening in the world. At the same time, this posture guards ethics against accommodating itself to the world's standards. God's activity in Christ sets humanity free to live "in the world without surrendering to its confining and desultory loyalties and temptations."[41] God's incarnational activity calls us to accept the world as a gift and to live in a spirit of gratitude. Such gratitude requires that we neither reject the gift nor use it for purposes at odds with divine intention.

Second, the incarnational character of divine activity has an integrative effect, bringing humanity to God, human beings to one another, and establishing an integrated sense of self. At the heart of this integration is the coming together of human beings who were once estranged from one another.[42] This understanding of divine activity leads Lehmann to make maturity a central feature of his ethic (a concept discussed in Chapter One). By Christian maturity Lehmann means "self-acceptance through self-giving."[43] Maturity, therefore, always involves the individual, but the individual understood in the context of community. Lehmann claims that according to the New Testament, " 'Maturity' means 'human wholeness,' the full or complete development of man as an individual and of all men in their

41. Ibid., p. 51.

42. As a result of the Incarnation and the continuing activity of the Spirit, the breach in human fellowship is healed, as Lehmann points out: "The demands of God became the bearer of God's claim upon men to be open towards one another and to behave towards one another as God, in Jesus the Messiah, had made plain that He was open and behaving towards them" ("The New Morality," p. 52). The incarnational thrust of Lehmann's method is meant to integrate the life of the believer with that of other believers, with that of nonbelievers, with that of the church, and with that of the world. It is meant to integrate the ways of God and human response.

43. Lehmann, *Ethics in a Christian Context* (New York: Harper & Row, 1963), p. 16. All subsequent references to this volume will be made parenthetically in the text.

relations with one another" (*Ethics*, p. 16). Lehmann's under-standing of belonging provides one example of maturity as self-giving. Although by "belonging" he means the sexual relation-ship between a man and a woman, his description of it illustrates what he means by Christian maturity.[44]

To "belong" in a relationship with another involves three things: identity, freedom, and fidelity. First, belonging to another requires a free act of self-giving to another self; this self-giving, however, arises from "a center of unified and stable selfhood," from an individual with a fully formed identity, and the act of self-giving is directed toward one who "is similarly centered, unified and stable." Belonging also requires that the gift of selfhood be given freely, "without dissimulation or self-justifi-cation." Finally, belonging involves receiving oneself as a gift from another who has also received you.[45] "Thus," according to Lehmann, "belonging is the human and humanizing presupposi-tion and power of involvement."[46] Similarly, maturity involves unified and centered selves who give themselves to one another in the context of trust and freedom.

Third, incarnational theology understands that God's activ-ity is free. In Lehmann's words, God is bound *to* but not *by* what God has done in the past (*Ethics,* p. 73). Lehmann's interpreta-tion of the Decalogue helps explain this relationship between divine constancy and freedom. Lehmann believes that an ethic of absolute moral imperative challenges the freedom of God by binding God to each commandment. If the absolute command applies uniformly to every situation, God is never free to act otherwise. One can in fact claim that God does not need to act at all. Although God laid down the Commandments, God is

44. Lehmann, "A Christian Look at the Sexual Revolution," in *Sexual Ethics and Christian Responsibility: Some Divergent Views,* ed. John Charles Wynn (New York: Association Press, 1970), pp. 51-82.

45. This is how Lehmann expresses it: "Belonging is the experience of receiving yourself, as and where you are, as a gift from another who has similarly received you, and finding in everything around you so many different ways of saying 'thank you'" (ibid., pp. 72-73).

46. Ibid., p. 72.

essentially removed from the situation. In contrast, a contextual approach points to the Incarnation rather than to divine commands as expressing God's ongoing activity in history. Through the Commandments, God has *described* responsible human existence. God is bound *to* these Commandments in that they constitute part of God's history with humanity; they are brought to each situation. However, God is not bound *by* them because each situation holds the possibility of a different response from God. The Commandments, therefore, do not constitute the *whole* of divine activity.

Lehmann believes that acknowledging the concrete, integrative (community-creating), and free nature of divine action steers ethics away from both absolutism and antinomianism. First, an absolutist ethic claims that the answer to the question "What should I do?" is always supplied by an ideal, a value, or a law that allows no exceptions. An absolute, Lehmann says, is "a standard of conduct which can be and must be applied to all people in all situations in exactly the same way" (*Ethics*, p. 125). In so defining ethical absolutism, he has been accused of fighting a straw opponent. No one, his critics claim, has ever proposed an absolute ethic in the way Lehmann describes it. Paul Ramsey, for instance, claims that "if that is the meaning of absolutes in ethics . . . then very few absolutists in ethical theory have measured up to it, and almost no defenders of moral principles have done so."[47] In response to this criticism, Lehmann describes the ethical absolutism that he opposes:

> The argument of the book [*Ethics in a Christian Context*] is that there is an absolutist tradition which goes back at least as far as Plato, that this tradition gave normative ethical significance to an overarching ethical idea, the idea of the Good, that this

47. Ramsey, "The Contextualism of Paul Lehmann," in *Deeds and Rules in Christian Ethics* (Lanham, Md.: University Press of America, 1983), pp. 76ff. Harmon L. Smith concurs, saying that so far as he is aware, ethical absolutes "are no longer serious options for most modern moralists." See Smith's book review of *Ethics in a Christian Context* in the *Duke Divinity School Review* 29-30 (Spring 1964-65): 142.

idea functioned as a standard of conduct which was to be applied to all people in all situations in the same way, [and] that precisely this functioning encountered the difficulty of the variety and complexity of actual ethical decision.[48]

Lehmann is puzzled by his critics' claim that the ethical absolutism which he opposes is simply a mirage. He complains that "the exponents of a 'normative ethic' are to be allowed to deny everything."[49] He claims that an ethic of moral absolutes does exist and necessitates clear opposition by those who believe ethical absolutism is a misinterpretation of the gospel.

In addition to rejecting ethical absolutism, Lehmann also seeks to avoid ethical antinomianism.[50] Because he believes that no principle can be identified as an absolute criterion of what is moral, his approach shares similarities with antinomianism. It differs from the antinomian approach, however, in that he believes that all factors in an ethical situation are related to the action of God, which brings about humanization. Lehmann does not propose that we enter each ethical situation with nothing other than a willingness to listen to the exigencies of the moment. Rather, he urges that we bring to each situation an understanding of what God has done for us, the identity and maturity which the church has fostered in us, and an understanding of what we "as believers in Jesus Christ and members of his Church" are to do.

Although Lehmann opposes an ethic of absolute law, he does not, as some critics suspect, suspend moral law altogether. After the publication of *Ethics in a Christian Context*, Lehmann promised to write another volume that would address the place the Commandments hold for Christian ethics. While portions of that manuscript have been published as two essays, the man-

---

48. Lehmann, "Comments on a Critique: Reply to Paul Ramsey," *Theology Today* 22, no. 1 (Apr. 1965): 123. This article was written in response to Paul Ramsey's critique of *Ethics in a Christian Context,* which appeared in the January issue of *Theology Today.*

49. Lehmann, "Comments on a Critique," p. 122.

50. Responsible human behavior, he says, demands some structure or framework (*Ethics,* p. 203).

uscript itself, currently titled "The Decalogue and a Human Future," is still in process.[51] Nevertheless, Lehmann's ongoing work focusing on the significance of the Decalogue challenges the charge that he promotes an antinomian position devoid of any directives for Christian behavior. In this work, Lehmann asserts that a Christian understanding of humanization requires that human beings be perceived as both limited and free; certain limits, in fact, create the very freedom that being human requires. The Ten Commandments are a significant source of those limits that produce freedom. Essential to understanding the nature of the Commandments is the notion that the laws are *descriptive* rather than *prescriptive*. Laws, in other words, *describe* the world as created and redeemed by God.[52]

Three Meanings of "Context." James Gustafson points out that there are three ways in which Lehmann uses the word "context" in his explication of Christian theological ethics. First, Lehmann uses it to refer to what God is doing in the world. As we have already seen, Lehmann believes that the politics of God provides the context for responsible human behavior. Second, Lehmann uses the word to refer to the specific situation in which God acts and the Christian responds. Third, Lehmann uses "context" to refer to the Christian community, the *koinonia*.[53]

51. Lehmann, "The Decalogue and the Parameters of a Human Future," paper delivered at the 1981 ACPE Conference entitled "Making and Keeping Human Life Human" (New York: ACPE Interchurch Center, 1981), p. 2. See also "The Commandments and the Common Life," *Interpretation*, Oct. 1980, pp. 341-55.

52. Lehmann, "The Decalogue and the Parameters of a Human Future." For a fuller discussion of Lehmann's understanding of the place the Ten Commandments hold in Christian ethics, see Chapter Four.

53. Gustafson, "Context vs. Principles," pp. 181-82. As pointed out previously, Joseph Fletcher is annoyed that Lehmann "muddies the waters" by using the word "context" to refer to the setting in which ethics is done as well as to the specific situation of an ethical decision. Paul Ramsey, on the other hand, has no objection to the claim that ethics is written in the context of Christian faith, although he, like Fletcher, believes the statement is self-evident. However, Ramsey does argue that there is no justification for moving from the claim that one does "ethics in a Christian context" to the claim that "Christian ethics is contextual." Ramsey describes Leh-

(1) *The Politics of God.* The etymology of the word "ethics," as discussed at the beginning of the previous chapter, points to the idea that ethics "is concerned with that which holds human society together" (*Ethics,* p. 25). It has to do with the security and stability necessary to make responsible human action possible. Lehmann does not arrive at this understanding purely from the etymology of the word "ethics." Rather, his reading of the biblical account of God's dealings with humanity shows that God's Incarnation in Jesus Christ was meant for the humanization (redemption) of sinful humanity. Thus at any given moment God calls us as creatures, redeemed sinners, and children of God into humanizing relationships with one another. This is the linchpin of Christian ethics:

> It is this *human factor* in the interrelationships of men which is the definitely ethical factor. A Christian ethic seeks to show that the human in us all can be rightly discerned and adhered to only in and through the reality of a climate of trust established by the divine humanity of Jesus Christ and the new humanity, however incipient, of all men in Christ. (*Ethics,* p. 130)

It is this humanizing activity of God, not the "calculated consistency" of applied principles or laws, that prevents a contextual ethics from leading to ethical anarchy (*Ethics,* pp. 131, 133).

(2) *The Specific Situation.* It is the Incarnation — that is, the historical specificity of God's action in the world — that leads Lehmann to emphasize historically specific situations for ethical concern. Quoting Bonhoeffer, Lehmann agrees that "whoever says 'God' cannot ignore the given world in which he lives, otherwise he would not be speaking the truth, otherwise he would not be speaking of the God who became incarnate in the world in Jesus Christ" (*Ethics,* p. 130). Lehmann finds political and sociological analysis of the situation — a knowledge of the facts — important for Christian moral action, but not the whole

---

mann's ethics as "act-*koinonia* ethics" (Ramsey, "The Contextualism of Paul Lehmann," pp. 74-75, 52).

of what is required. Humanizing activity is always the goal of any given decision, whether the situation involves a very serious ethical dilemma, such as whether to perform an abortion, or the most mundane action, such as selling a car. The specific situation requires discovering the "significant in the factual." Wanting to sell a car, for instance, is the fact; the buyer and the seller discovering each other's humanity — perhaps through the seller being honest with the buyer — is the significant goal (*Ethics*, p. 130). The specific situation provides the context for witnessing to the humanizing activity of God in Jesus Christ.

(3) *The Christian Koinonia.* Lehmann says that the Christian response to the ethical question "What am I as a believer in Jesus Christ and a member of his church to do?" has most often been "I am to do the will of God." That in turn raises the question "How do I know what the will of God is?" In Lehmann's view we apprehend the will of God within the context of the *koinonia*, the "community-creating reality of Jesus Christ." Within the *koinonia* we understand that the will of God is "that which makes and keeps human life human":

> It is in the *koinonia* that one comes in sight of and finds oneself involved in what God is doing in the world. What God is doing is setting up and carrying out the conditions for what it takes to keep human life human. The fruit of this activity is human maturity inaugurated and being fulfilled by Jesus Christ in the world. The description of this activity of God provides a *koinonia* ethic with its biblical and theological foundations. (*Ethics*, p. 123)

According to Lehmann, the *koinonia* is the primary context for Christian ethics. Here the word and action of God in Jesus Christ take visible form, leading to human maturity and human response to divine action.

Criticisms. Two consistent criticisms have been aimed at contextualism in general and at Paul Lehmann's contextualism specifically. The first criticism charges that contextualism, as a product of the time in which it arose, accommodates behavior to the exigencies of the moment. The second charge is that contextualism, by virtue of its antinomian posture, has a "piecemeal" character which lacks continuity from one ethical situation to the next.

In their charge of accommodation, critics claim that contextual ethicists have yielded to the secular mood of the times and in the process have been untrue to the tenets of Christianity, that they have employed a secular interpretation of contextualism rather than identifying a genuine Christian characteristic of ethics. Paul Ramsey, for instance, claims contextualism is "non-biblical," "non-theological," and "disturbing to anyone concerned with Christian ethics."[54]

This criticism often results from reflection on the historical circumstances out of which contextualism arose. Critics insist that contextual ethics has no lasting significance apart from the dire circumstances that brought it about. The rejection of universal principles along with the extreme emphasis on the situation, critics claim, is strictly a "product of external conditions," having arisen during the perilous times of World War II:

> Problems of cooperating with the invading conquerors, of joining resistance movements, of the black market, of retaliation, of avoiding torture, of professing the faith in the face of diabolical persecution, of observing rigid laws of conjugal morality in the midst of the most dire poverty, of having children who would be just so much "gun fodder," of preserving premarital chastity when almost every form of innocent entertainment seems beyond the reach of youth — these and countless other difficult problems became a part of the very atmosphere created by the war and its aftermath.[55]

Given the reign of horror of Nazi Germany, when dire circumstances and moral dilemmas became everyday occurrences, the

---

54. Ramsey, "The Contextualism of Paul Lehmann," p. 50. Ramsey frequently charges Lehmann with using the language and ideas of nontheological humanism.

55. Ford and Kelly, *Contemporary Moral Theology*, p. 125.

rise of contextualism is understandable, critics say: "With this dark picture in mind, it will be easy to see why the various tendencies that came to be known as 'situation ethics,' and that stem from existentialism, could be fostered."[56] However, these critics believe that this observation provides a justification for dismissing the validity of the contextual approach to ethics. Contextualism works well only in dire circumstances, they say, and has no lasting effect on day-to-day living.

But this criticism is misguided on two accounts. First, it concedes that an ethic of absolute principles or rules only inadequately addresses the demands of dire situations. While deductive ethics can guide people through everyday dilemmas, it fails in the straits, its proponents admit. This is a bigger concession than the defenders of an ethic of absolute laws should want to make. Second, this criticism implies that dire ethical dilemmas are uncommon, occurring usually in the context of catastrophes such as war. There is no recognition that when a particular community experiences relatively calm circumstances free of tragedy or injustice, it has a responsibility to act in solidarity with other communities that *are* experiencing turmoil and persecution. There has never been a time in history when people were not faced with the task of "professing the faith in the face of diabolical persecution." If an ethic of principles is inadequate when one directly experiences such persecution, then it is also inadequate when one stands beside those who are experiencing such injustice.

Like other defenders of contextualism, Lehmann admits that the historical setting is an important factor in the rise of this method. After all, the method itself urges one to listen to the facts of the particular environment in which one is called to decisive action. Nevertheless, in developing his ethic Lehmann believes he has not simply accommodated Christian ethics to a concept that arose during difficult times:

It cannot be too strongly stressed that the contextual character of Christian ethics . . . is derived from the ethical reality and

56. Ibid.

significance of the Christian *koinonia*. The contextual character
of Christian ethics is not derived from an application to the
Christian *koinonia* of a general theory of contextualism. (*Ethics,*
pp. 14-15)[57]

Lehmann has not emphasized the contextual character of ethics
simply as an effort to be up-to-date with the rise of existentialism
in the 1940s, with the dire circumstances created by World
War II, or with the rebellious times of the 1960s. Rather, he has
developed this emphasis because he subscribes to an incarnational theology, and an incarnational theology — which holds
that God's action in Jesus Christ has significance in history,
including the present moment of history — will respond to, not
accommodate itself to and certainly not withdraw from, rebellious times. It will seek to find signs of God's activity in the
midst of political events.

A second common criticism of contextual ethics is that its
various proponents offer only piecemeal presentations of moral
action. If prescriptive norms cannot anticipate what one is to
do in advance of the actual situation, then moral decision-
making is always moment to moment, with no connecting tissue
to tie the various moments together. Against this criticism one
can claim that all contextualists identify *some* factor that provides continuity from one moral situation to the next. Even
Sartre, the most radically antinomian ethicist, finds continuity
in the concept of human freedom. Fletcher finds continuity in
wedding *agape* to utilitarianism. And Barth, Hauerwas, and Lehmann hold that the continuity is provided by the story of God's
action in relation to human creatures.

John Bennett, however, claims that these various connecting
factors identified by contextualists are really nothing more than
references to general rules or principles. In short, Bennett
believes that contextualists are doing the very thing they claim
to oppose. In fact, he believes that it is impossible to develop a
contextual ethic completely divorced from "normative" consid-

57. See also "Comments on a Critique," p. 121.

erations.[58] When faced with a particular moral dilemma, he says, one is always confronted with "broad religious and ethical interpretations which come from outside the situation."[59] Therefore, Bennett claims, the risk of contextual ethics lies in falling into a piecemeal, sporadic ethic that relies wholly on each specific situation. Furthermore, those contextualists who avoid this error do so by relying on the very thing they set out to overthrow: general principles.

While Bennett is correct in pointing out the possible danger of contextual ethics, he is incorrect in his charge of the inconsistency necessary to prevent or correct the danger. It is true, for instance, that Lehmann does not approach each specific situation in a vacuum: he speaks out of faith in God's action in Jesus Christ. According to Lehmann, analysis of the specific ethical situation alone does not provide what is needed to make a decision — that is, it does not provide what is necessary to hold human life together. Nor, however, do absolute rules, principles, laws, and so forth hold human life together. If in asserting that contextualists use "general principles" Bennett is referring to statements of faith out of which the contextual ethics is built, then it is true that Lehmann holds "general principles." Bennett, however, does not acknowledge that there is an important difference between claiming that the connecting factor between one situation and the next lies in the activity of God, as Lehmann does, and claiming that it lies in general principles of behavior, as Bennett does. Accordingly, the fundamental question that must be asked regarding Lehmann's ethics is what he means when he says "God acts." No aspect of Lehmann's ethic is clear without an explanation of this claim.

58. Bennett, "Principles and the Situation," p. 9.
59. Ibid., p. 25.

III

Lehmann's Interpretation of Revelation and Story

According to Lehmann, the primary task of theological ethics is to discern what God is doing in the world. "Humanization" and the "politics of God," the *koinonia*, "parabolic action," the "contextual" nature of Christian ethics — all these concepts hinge on the intelligibility of Lehmann's claim that "God acts." In Lehmann's interpretation of divine action we find both the heart of his theology and the need for further clarification. Given the charge from critics that Lehmann's ethic relies on "instant discernment," one must ask if "divine politics" offers a substantial category for ethics.

By raising the question of what Lehmann means when he says "God acts," we stumble upon a fundamental issue for Christian faith and theology: the nature of divine revelation and the appropriate mode of human speech about God. Here we arrive at the heart of the task and the dilemma of Christian theology. Lehmann's focus on the action of God sets him in the thicket of an ongoing theological debate. I will address his interpretation of the claim that "God acts" in this chapter and the next, first by examining the concepts of revelation and story and then by examining the concept of apocalyptic.

Theology and Revelation

Early in his theological career, Gordon Kaufman pointed out that while the claim "God acts" marks an indispensable characteristic of Christian faith, it also presents a problem for post-Enlightenment thinkers.[1] The problem arises because scientific thought has shifted our focus from a "created" to a "natural" world. What was once described as a world created and sustained by God is now understood as a world that is self-generating and self-sustaining. Reference to natural causes for events has replaced reference to divine causes. According to Kaufmann, that contemporary thought no longer refers to God's intervention in the natural order completely contradicts the biblical understanding of divine acts visible in nature.[2]

Kaufman points out that one cannot remedy this problem by shifting the locus of divine activity from nature to history.[3] Not only is it impossible to separate nature and history into two unrelated realms, but the contemporary discipline of history, just like the study of nature, has its own scientific explanations for the causes and effects of historical events that operate without recourse to the concept of divine action.[4]

Once we admit that we can no longer speak of God as agent in the sense that God intervenes in the processes of nature or history, Kaufman says we must choose among three alternatives: (1) we can admit that the idea of divine agency is so necessary to our

1. Kaufman, *God the Problem* (Cambridge: Harvard University Press, 1972), p. xi.
2. Ibid., p. 121.
3. Kaufman says, "It will not do to speak of God as the agent who made it possible for the Israelites to escape from the Egyptians, if one regards it as simply a fortunate coincidence that a strong east wind was blowing at just the right time to dry up the sea of reeds. The biblical writer's view is coherent and compelling precisely because he is able to say that 'the Lord drove the sea back by a strong east wind' (Exod. 14:21); that is, it was because, and only because, God was Lord over nature, one who could bend natural events to his will, that he was able to be effective Lord over history" (*God the Problem*, p. 122).
4. Ibid., p. 123.

doctrine of God that if agency is dismissed, the concept of God is dismissed as well; (2) we can redefine our doctrine of God so that the claim "God acts" is *not* an essential aspect of it; or (3) we can redefine the word "acts" so that we can retain the notion that "God acts" without claiming that God's action interrupts the natural or historical order. Early in his career Kaufman accepted this third alternative. Recently, however, he has embraced the second alternative, redefining God apart from the claim that "God acts."

According to Ronald Thiemann, Kaufman now replaces the concept of God as a "transcendent agent" with the more Kantian notion of God as a "transcendental ideal." Kaufman defines the function of theology solely by "epistemological considerations," whereby theology becomes purely theoretical and constructive.[5] He develops his theology, therefore, without recourse to the concept of revelation.

Revelation according to the Enlightenment and Liberalism. Theology without revelation, Paul Lehmann claims, is one of the major legacies of Enlightenment and liberal theology. He identifies three characteristics of eighteenth- and nineteenth-century thought that undermine revelation as a necessary category for

---

5. Thiemann summarizes Kaufman's more recent position:

    a. Theology has no access to a transcendent divine being, and thus its claims can neither be founded upon nor authorized by an appeal to divine revelation.

    b. Theology has no given content to describe, and its concepts do not correspond to a transcendent reality; theology is a purely constructive activity of the human imagination.

    c. Theological concepts are constructed not primarily from the parochial tradition of a particular religious community but from the linguistic heritage of the broader cultural community.

    d. The word "God" does not refer or correspond to a transcendent being who is the object of theological knowledge; rather, "God" functions as the focal point of an all-encompassing framework of interpretation.

    e. The criteria by which theological claims are to be assessed are not those of correspondence but are thoroughly pragmatic in character.

Thiemann, *Revelation and Theology: A Theological Inquiry* (University Park: Pennsylvania State University Press, 1987), p. 51.

theology: (1) the triumph of human reason, (2) the doctrine of polarity, and (3) the reduction of religion to a moral code.[6] It will be helpful to look at each of these characteristics individually.

(1) *The Triumph of Human Reason.* Reacting against the rigidity of theological orthodoxy, the Enlightenment sought to free human reason to pursue knowledge even when knowledge countered the church's claims for revelation. Although Lehmann criticizes many of the consequences of this move, he reminds us of our debt to the Enlightenment and to the liberal movement in theology because it freed reason for the pursuit of knowledge and truth.

According to Lehmann, problems arose because liberating reason from the church's fear of the truth was not enough for Enlightenment thought. The complete triumph of reason over revelation increasingly became its goal. Whereas the medieval synthesis of the Catholic Church had maintained two avenues to truth (reason and science on the one hand, revelation and faith on the other), the rationalism of the Enlightenment began to set aside revelation to ever-greater degrees (*Forgiveness*, p. 17).

This triumph of reason, Lehmann says, led to the claim that human beings, by virtue of their natural capacity to reason, can acquire the knowledge of God and of God's will necessary for responsible human action. In such an understanding, divine revelation clearly "has no tenure of its own." According to Lehmann, this reliance on reason grew steadily until, by the middle of the eighteenth century, many philosophers and theologians disregarded revelation as an avenue to truth (*Forgiveness*, pp.16-17).

Even when Christian theology sought to establish the validity of divine revelation, it failed to carry its convictions very far. Reason always cast a shadow over the reliability of claims based on revelation. Evidence for the validity of revelation could be demonstrated if it were the fulfillment of prophecy, or if it were

6. Lehmann, *Forgiveness: Decisive Issue in Protestant Thought* (New York: Harper & Brothers, 1940), pp. 20, 37.

accompanied by a "visible sign" in the form of a miracle. Accordingly, arguments from fulfilled prophecy and miracle were the last weak pegs in defense of revelation (*Forgiveness*, p. 23).

It seems puzzling that an age which placed so much emphasis on reason would find any credibility in the concept of miracle. The argument from miracle, however, was itself a well-reasoned position that allowed room for a *rational* acceptance of the idea of revelation.

According to Ronald Thiemann, John Locke set the stage for defending revelation through the argument from miracle in his *Essay Concerning Human Understanding*. Reason, he said, usually demands the aid of intuition and deduction in order to acknowledge that something is true. Because divinely revealed truth is not susceptible to intuition or deduction, Locke provided the grounds for reason's assent to the truth of divine revelation through the idea of "the credit of the proposer."[7] According to this concept, faith can reasonably accept the truth of a proposition if that truth can be demonstrated to come from God, who, as "the proposer" of the truth, would have unquestionable credibility. One must, however, provide reasonable evidence that the proposition is indeed from God. This reasonable evidence is discovered in "God's extraordinary way of communication" — that is, through miracle.[8]

Inevitably, the arguments from miracle and fulfilled prophecy could not hold up under critical examination. David Hume, in the name of philosophy, and Friedrich Schleiermacher, in the name of Christian theology, rejected the arguments from miracle and fulfilled prophecy as unreasonable. In the meantime, the Enlightenment pursuit of knowledge had set into motion concepts of religion and God that functioned apart from the doctrine

---

7. Thiemann, *Revelation and Theology*, p. 17.

8. Hence the Age of Reason relied on what is now considered unreasonable evidence — that is, miraculous acts. Fundamentalism often does not acknowledge that its focus on divine miracle is an inheritance from this rationalistic stance of the Enlightenment, an inheritance from philosophers and theologians who found it difficult to believe in divine revelation.

of revelation (*Forgiveness*, p. 20). In the upholding of such concepts of religion and God, the notion of humanity as *animale rationale* — a concept that Lehmann has spent much of his career fighting against — reached the peak of its influence.

(2) *The Doctrine of Polarity.* The doctrine of polarity suggests that though there is certainly a distinction between God and humanity, the distinction is not one of an unfathomable gulf but one of polarity. God and humanity exist at opposite ends of the same pole. This description of the "polar relation" of the nature of God and the nature of humanity is bolstered by the claim of natural theology that reason is the "point of contact" at which the human and divine natures intersect. Lehmann explains the concept:

> In good Greek fashion, the divine and the human have the same fundamental nature, the inherent rationality of the soul. . . . It is as though God and man were at opposite ends of a pole. The pole is the reason, which, as the unifying principle (nature) underlying all change and variation, is common to them both. The pole has *two* ends, to be sure, but they are, nevertheless, ends of the *same* pole. (*Forgiveness*, p. 20)

This resulted in a blurring of the distinction between divine and human nature, and a consequent tendency to worship humanity, though the Enlightened Deists clearly did not intend that result. Lehmann points out that Descartes was among the first to set forth this doctrine of polarity.

Descartes, in agreement with the Reformers before him, claimed that human knowledge of God comes as a gift to humanity from God.[9] According to Ronald Thiemann, in setting out

---

9. Thiemann quotes Descartes's letter to the theological faculty of Paris: "It is absolutely true, both that we must believe that there is a God because it is taught in the Holy Scriptures, and, on the other hand, that we must believe the Holy Scriptures because they come from God. The reason for this is that faith is a gift of God, and the very God that gives us the faith to believe other things can also give us the faith to believe that he exists" (*Theology and Revelation*, p. 12).

to demonstrate the proof of this claim, Descartes asserted that an argument concerning the human ego ("I think; therefore I am") was necessary to establish arguments for the existence of God. Thus, although Descartes may have claimed that divine reality is ontologically prior to human existence, he justified that claim by using an argument concerning the nature of humanity.[10] According to Lehmann, this involves an attempt to demonstrate "the validity of the claims of faith on the basis of a general knowledge of [humanity] and the world" (*Forgiveness*, p. 10).

Almost two hundred years after Descartes, Friedrich Schleiermacher initiated the liberal theological tradition of the nineteenth century. His Christian anthropology, which described religion as an irreducible dimension of human life, is consistent with the doctrine of polarity. According to Schleiermacher, all human beings have a sense of absolute dependence on a being more powerful than themselves. Human beings have this feeling prior to any form of teaching or preaching; it constitutes part of the human makeup. Because this feeling of absolute dependence sets humanity in relation to God, one can claim that being in relationship with God constitutes a natural human capacity.

Schleiermacher's method, like that of Descartes, requires that one first understand the nature of humanity before one can understand the nature of God. Lehmann says that this method suggests that "to know what [humanity] is like, is already to know what God is like, since there is no distinction between them, save that between the part and the whole" (*Forgiveness*, p. 44). Revelation is no longer conceived as solely an act of God; it is also a universal human possibility. God's self-revealing act begins not only with God but also as an innate aspect of human nature.

Descartes' position in the seventeenth century and Schleiermacher's in the nineteenth century represent the consequences of what Thiemann calls "a decisive shift in sensibility" regarding the doctrine of revelation, a shift that occurred between the

10. Ibid., p. 13.

Reformation and the Enlightenment. The Reformers simply assumed that knowledge of God is possible based on divine revelation; Enlightenment theologians believed it necessary to justify their claims about God using the standards and tools of philosophy and epistemology. According to Thiemann, this shift from assuming to demonstrating the truth of divine revelation indicates that knowledge of God has become "a dependent belief . . . justified in relation to new basic convictions independent of the Christian faith."[11]

Lehmann says that the Enlightenment shift from assuming to demonstrating the truth of revelation did not indicate that Enlightenment thinkers had abandoned religion altogether. Even the Deists, who had abandoned the Christian faith, believed in a superior being. The religion that both the Deists and many Christian theologians defined, however, was one which held that human beings could obtain knowledge of God and God's will through their natural capacity for reason (*Forgiveness*, p. 16). In short, they sought to establish "rational religion," the religion of reason apart from revelation. This rational religion often entailed identifying morality as the essence of religion.

(3) *The Reduction of Religion to a Moral Code.* Beginning with the Enlightenment and continuing through nineteenth-century liberalism, philosophers and theologians located the essence of the religious faith in moral teaching. Christianity, it was often claimed, offered the best possible expression of morality.

Prior to the Enlightenment, Christian tradition based duty on religious belief. Immanuel Kant reversed this order, making the move *from* morality *to* religious faith, by replacing speculative proofs for the existence of God with a moral proof.[12] To understand the full impact of Kant's argument, one must recognize that Kant believed that morality constitutes not the essence

---

11. Thiemann, *Revelation and Theology*, p. 9.
12. Lehmann believes that Kant's movement from morality to religion and his moral proof for the existence of God exposed him as a "child of his time" more than any other aspect of his thought (*Forgiveness*, p. 37).

of *religion* but the essence of *human existence*. Accordingly, religion grows out of morality. Morality, therefore, actually does not need religion at all; rather, religion arises from pre-existing human morality. Thus, says Lehmann, Kant's moral proof for the existence of God raises the same question regarding religion as the whole of eighteenth-century rationalism: "Why, on these terms, believe in any God at all?" (*Forgiveness*, p. 40).

In 1944, Lehmann outlined five affirmations that the theology of his day had inherited from eighteenth- and nineteenth-century thought: (1) religion is not a matter of doctrine but a matter of life; (2) the value of religion lies in its social utility; (3) Christianity is the best of all religions because of its superior ethical vitality; (4) religious affirmations are valid only to the extent that they can be justified by human experience; and (5) "divine revelation is correlative with human discovery" (*Forgiveness*, p. 11). It was against such an inheritance that the theology of Karl Barth spoke a resounding "No!"

The Challenge to Enlightenment and Liberal Theology: Dialectical Theology. Against the doctrine of polarity, Barth claimed with Kierkegaard that there is an "infinite, qualitative distinction between time and eternity," between humanity and God.[13] Humanity can add nothing to divine revelation, because both divine revelation and the human ability to receive it are gifts from God. In agreement with the Reformers, Barth claimed that knowledge of humanity and knowledge of God cannot be separated. In opposition to nineteenth-century liberals, however, he asserted that the movement of knowledge was *from* God *to* humanity. No knowledge is uncovered by moving from human nature to divine nature. With this latter movement all knowledge is distorted and idolatrous. Barth claimed that we know who we are only because God has revealed who God is. Lehmann summarizes the doctrines that Barth believed were essential for theology:

(1) *The sovereign freedom of God.* God's sovereignty and

13. Barth, *The Epistle to the Romans*, trans. Edwyn C. Hoskyns (New York: Oxford University Press, 1968), pp. 98-99.

radical freedom mean that God is free both to reveal and to veil God's self in accordance with the mystery of divine being and action.[14]

(2) *God's self-revelation.* Barth believed that God's revelation does not consist of a moral code; what God reveals is God's self. Furthermore, this self-revelation is not an internal human experience but is always manifested through a physical event.

(3) *The Word of God.* God's revelation is best understood as God's "Word" to us. This revelation takes on a threefold form: Jesus Christ, the Bible, and Christian proclamation.

(4) *The crisis of human existence.* The relationship between God and humanity is characterized initially by crisis. The Word of God exposes humanity's true existence as rebellion against God. God and humanity do not exist at opposite ends of the same pole; a great gulf separates them, a gulf that can be crossed only by God. To achieve human wholeness, humanity must be radically transformed, a transformation that can be accomplished only by God.

(5) *The paradox.* Only paradoxical terms can describe the relation between God and humanity, because both God's activity and human existence are paradoxical. The paradox of God's activity is evident in the Incarnation, whereby Christ is fully God and fully human, and in God's justification of the ungodly. Human existence is paradoxical in that each person is both believer and unbeliever, child of death and child of life.

In 1944 Lehmann described himself as standing at the juncture between "the gradual disintegration of liberalism" and "the still uncertain ascendancy of the dialectical movement." While he rejected what he believed was the heart of nineteenth-century thought (the triumph of reason, the doctrine of polarity, and the reduction of Christianity to a system of morals), he believed that liberal theology rightly affirmed the goodness of creation and God's concrete activity in history and nature by stressing

14. Lehmann, "The Theology of Crisis," in *The Twentieth-Century Encyclopedia of Religious Knowledge,* ed. Lefferts A. Loetscher (Grand Rapids: Baker Publishing House, 1955), p. 311.

the "historical character of Christ's mediation" (*Forgiveness*, p. 172).

Although Lehmann embraced dialectical theology's affirmation of the radical distinction between God and humanity, he was critical of its tendency to isolate divine revelation outside the human world of "time and space and things." Lehmann saw a dangerous tendency toward this ahistorical posture in Barth's early doctrine of God; he believed that Barth had lost sight of his own dialectical method for describing the nature of divine activity and was in danger of removing God from human history altogether.

Lehmann had no objection to Barth's radical dismissal of "even the minutest human potentiality" for the reception of divine grace (*Forgiveness*, p. 190). He did, however, object to the diminished value he believed Barth's early writings gave to the doctrine of creation. While liberal theology dissolved the tension between the doctrine of creation and the doctrine of redemption, Lehmann thought Barth's early work placed too wide a gulf between them. He feared that Barth had ceased to write "between the times" and was in danger of writing "above the times"; what Lehmann wanted to do was to hold the doctrines of creation and redemption together. The close connection between these two doctrines continues to characterize all of Lehmann's work.

Maintaining a close connection between these two doctrines shapes Lehmann's theological and ethical method, a method also shaped by his interpretation of Calvin's understanding of the relationship between knowledge of God and knowledge of humanity. Lehmann agrees with Calvin that knowledge of God and knowledge of humanity are interrelated. Knowledge of who we are and what our destiny is as human beings requires a knowledge of divine sovereignty. As Lehmann points out, Calvin did not completely disallow the possibility of beginning with the knowledge of "human things." This course necessitated neither the rejection of revelation nor the proposal that revelation forms an innate characteristic of humanity. Nevertheless, though Calvin allowed for the possibility of beginning with "human things," he began with the knowledge of God. Lehmann suggests an alternative: rather than moving from "Scripture to knowledge of God in Christ," we can move from "Scripture to knowledge of human things in Christ." That Scripture is still the beginning of knowledge places revelation prior to human nature.

Lehmann believes this change of emphasis has an impact on both Christian anthropology and the doctrine of God. Liberal theology distorted Christian anthropology by emphasizing the human capacity for natural knowledge of God. With this emphasis true humanity is given up because the connection between knowledge of God and humanity is lost. When one begins with the knowledge of humanity, one never fully reaches knowledge of God. Accordingly, one speaks of humanity apart from God.

According to Lehmann, Barth's early theology distorted the doctrine of God by emphasizing God's transcendence at the expense of divine immanence. Calvin's connection between knowledge of God and knowledge of humanity went awry from the other direction. When one begins with the knowledge of God, one never fully reaches the knowledge of humanity. Accordingly, one speaks of God apart from humanity.

Lehmann wants to start with knowledge of God *and* emphasize knowledge of humanity. At the heart of his theological method for ethics lies his constant attempt to keep these two emphases together.[15] This attempt explains two important characteristics of Lehmann's theology of revelation.

First, in seeking to maintain the right relation between knowledge of God and knowledge of humanity, Lehmann iden-

---

15. "As the Reformers saw it, revelation and faith came to life in the reality of a dynamic inter-relation between the initiative of God and the concrete acts of men in response to this initiative." According to Lehmann, these two kinds of acts — the acts of God and the acts of humanity — cannot be separated ("On Doing Theology: A Contextual Possibility," in *Prospect for Theology: Essays in Honour of H. H. Farmer,* ed. F. G. Healey [Welwyn Garden City, Eng.: James Nisbet & Co., 1966], p. 133).

tifies the church as the place where they coincide. That Lehmann starts with the Christian church in developing his theology of revelation indicates that while he begins with God's revelation, it is revelation always understood concretely in human history. The church is God's revelation in concrete, historical form. Lehmann's understanding of the transcendence of God is always matched by a simultaneous affirmation of God's immanence. Although he clearly begins with revelation and Christology, by using the Christian church as the starting point for theological ethics he unites both Christology and anthropology, God's action and human response. Lehmann unites them not in a way that confuses or confounds them, but in such a way that one cannot speak about one without being led to examine the other.

Second, Lehmann's attempt to keep a close connection between the doctrines of creation and redemption clarifies why his theology lacks a well-developed Christology even though Christology is the initiating doctrine. While he does not want to *begin* with the doctrine of humanity, he is anxious to move quickly into a discussion of what it means to be human. Lehmann's approach is founded on a Christology but concentrates on the definition of humanity that grows out of it. In his eagerness to discuss "that which makes and keeps human life human," Lehmann presupposes rather than details a strong Christology.

In light of Lehmann's interpretation of the doctrine of revelation, we turn now to explore how the concept of "story" helps define what he means when he claims that "God acts."

Theology and Story

According to Langdon Gilkey, contemporary theologians have rendered claims for God's action unintelligible by attempting to couch a modern worldview in biblical and orthodox language. This attempt seeks to maintain claims for the "space-time continuum" (God does *not* interrupt the laws of nature) while *also* maintaining claims for the "mighty acts of God" in nature.[16] Gilkey argues that it is impossible to put the content of liberal theology in orthodox dress.

Gilkey says we avoid this anachronistic error by recognizing

16. Gilkey addresses the fact that in the history of Christian thought there are at least two opposing claims made regarding divine action. On the one hand, the claim that "God acts" can indicate the belief that God suspends the natural order, thereby producing "miraculous" events. This was the "orthodox" view of the eighteenth century, a view still held by Christian fundamentalists today. The liberal tradition, on the other hand, maintains that to say "God acts" should never suggest that God suspends the laws of nature. Rather, it indicates that faith discerns the activity of God in events of nature, even though those events have perfectly natural explanations. In the first case the claim that "God acts" becomes incredible; in the second case the claim that "God acts" borders on the inconsequential.

The first approach uses theological language to describe God's action in a univocal way — that is, it attaches literal correspondence to claims for divine action. Here the statement "God acts" refers to God's voice being audible to human ears and to acts of God visible to human eyes. This interpretation recognizes little or no discrepancy between what human language describes God as doing and what God actually does.

The second approach uses theological language to describe God's action in an equivocal way. On the one hand, equivocal means "capable of two interpretations." This is, after all, what those who hold this view are claiming. Apart from faith, one interprets an event in one way, whereas with faith one interprets it in another. On the other hand, however, "equivocal" means "ambiguous," "evasive," or "cryptic." In this sense equivocal language suggests almost no correspondence between claims for divine action and what God actually does. The discrepancy between human language and divine action is so vast that language about God becomes almost meaningless.

Gilkey has charged that contemporary theology falls into the error of equivocal language in this negative sense. He asks, " 'Are the main words and categories in biblical theology meaningful?' If they are no longer used univocally to mean observable deeds and audible voices, do they have any intelligible content? If they are in fact being used as analogies (God acts, but not as men act; God speaks, but not with an audible voice), do we have any idea at all to what sort of deed or communication these analogies refer? Or are they just serious-sounding, biblical-sounding, and theological-sounding words to which we can, if pressed, assign no meaning?" ("Cosmology, Ontology, and the Travail of Biblical Language," *Journal of Religion* 41 [1961]: 199. See also Christopher L. Morse, "Raising God's Eyebrows: Some Further Thoughts on the *Analogia Fidei*," *Union Seminary Quarterly Review* 37, nos. 1 & 2 [Fall/Winter 1981-82]: 39-50).

that when we say "God acts," we do not mean the same thing the biblical writers meant. Whereas the biblical writers referred literally to wondrous acts performed by God and God speaking audibly to humans, we reject such literal references. Given this rejection, Gilkey claims the terms "God speaks" and "God acts" demand a more specific definition shaped by the discipline of philosophical theology.

Although Gilkey accurately describes the church's tendency toward literal interpretation of biblical descriptions of God's actions, his analysis falls short in its understanding of the intention of the biblical writers themselves. On what grounds does he assume that the writers of biblical literature *did not know* they were writing stories rather than liberal firsthand accounts of divine actions? Why does he so readily assume that what we mean when we say "God acts" is radically different from what the writers J, E, D, and P meant?[17]

The biblical theologian Robert Alter claims that biblical writers not only knew they were writing stories instead of first-person accounts; they also consciously employed all the play-fulness and skill of any great storyteller.[18] Not only did they interpret historical events, argues Alter; they sometimes *created* events out of their own literary imaginations. There is no evidence to support Gilkey's claim that when these writers said that "God spoke" or "God acted," they claimed to be referring to an audible voice or a visible event.[19] Surely the writers of the two

---

17. Gilkey, "Cosmology, Ontology, and the Travail of Biblical Language," p. 204.

18. Alter, *The Art of Biblical Narrative* (New York: Basic Books, 1981).

19. Alter's position runs completely counter to that given by Erich Auerbach in the popular book *Mimesis*. In comparing Homer's *Odyssey* to the biblical story of the sacrifice of Isaac, Auerbach claims that the Elohist who recorded the story of Isaac "had to believe" in the "object truth" of the story he told because "the existence of the sacred ordinances of life rested upon the truth of this and similar stories. He had to believe in it passionately; or else (as many rationalistic interpreters believed and perhaps still believe) he had to be a conscious liar — no harmless liar like Homer, who lied to give pleasure, but a political liar with a definite end in view, lying in the interest of a claim to absolute authority" (*The Art of Biblical Narrative*, p. 14).

creation stories in Genesis, for instance, did not pretend to be eyewitnesses to God's act of creation. Gilkey's observations correctly identify the fundamentalist tendency to *interpret* the Bible as eyewitness accounts of God's action, but he incorrectly assumes that the biblical writers themselves claimed such literal correspondence between what they wrote and what God did. When one acknowledges with Alter that the biblical writers *consciously* and *purposefully* intermingled fiction with nonfiction to describe the actions of God, one has begun to identify the importance that "story" holds for theology.

Lehmann stands among a growing number of theologians who seek to make sense out of the claim "God acts" by reference to the concept of "story." Over the last few decades scholarly research has yielded a variety of claims about the significance of story or narrative for systematic theology, theological ethics, biblical studies, and the study of religions. Current uses of story as a category for biblical and theological studies are so varied that critics believe the concept is threatened by an ambiguity that renders it useless.[20]

In an attempt to wrest some meaning from this confusion, we will examine the following: (1) the definition of story as

---

20. In spite of the ambiguity of the term, many scholars have continued to explore its usefulness as a biblical and theological category. George Stroup's book entitled *The Promise of Narrative Theology: Recovering the Gospel in the Church* provides one of the clearest descriptions of the various ways the term has been used and gives an account of his own proposal for its proper use. Stroup describes three forms of narrative theology: (a) Introduction to Religion, (b) Life-Story and Lived Convictions, and (c) Biblical Narrative ([Atlanta: John Knox Press, 1981], pp. 73-74). As examples, Stroup cites Sam Keen's *To a Dancing God* (New York: Harper & Row, 1970), Harvey Cox's *The Seduction of the Spirit* (New York: Simon & Schuster, 1974), Michael Novak's *Ascent of the Mountain, Flight of the Dove* (New York: Harper & Row, 1971), and Gabriel Fackre's *The Christian Story* (Grand Rapids: Wm. B. Eerdmans, 1978). Only the last of these attempts to discuss specific Christian doctrines in light of the category of narrative. Stroup finds these books lacking in precise definition of the concept they set out to discuss. A more recent collection of essays on narrative theology is *Why Narrative? Readings in Narrative Theology*, ed. Stanley Hauerwas and L. Gregory Jones (Grand Rapids: Eerdmans, 1989).

metaphor; (2) two approaches to the use of story, one arising out of claims for the narrative quality of human experience, the other out of claims for the narrative quality of divine revelation; and (3) how to measure the truth of narrative accounts. These explanations will be used to describe and evaluate the way Lehmann employs story. In light of these discussions we will return to the question of what Lehmann means when he says "God acts."

Story as Metaphor. In the pages that follow, "story" and "narrative" will be used interchangeably to designate any account that seeks to bring order to the relationship between the past, present, and future for individuals or communities.[21] Given this general description, "story" can be used literally to refer to a specific legend, myth, and so on, or it can be used in a broader, more metaphorical sense to refer to a collection of stories that, taken together, give a coherent account of the origins, development, and destiny of a person or group. This collection of stories can be referred to as "the story" of an individual or a people. The Bible, then, is a story that contains individual stories of origin (e.g., the creation stories in Genesis), development (e.g., the stories of the Fall, the history of Israel, the beginning of the church), and destiny (e.g., the stories of Jesus' life, death, and resurrection). This movement from origin to destiny can be said to form *one* story.

Those who rely on this broader interpretation of "story" believe that story provides the meaning and order necessary to protect life from chaos and insignificance.[22] Sam Keen illustrates this point by describing the use of story in preliterate culture:

Preliterate man lived in a world which received its intellectual, religious, and social structure through the story. Each tribe had its own set of tales, myths, and legends which defined the

21. Frank Kermode, *The Sense of an Ending: Studies in the Theology of Fiction* (New York: Oxford University Press, 1967), pp. 5, 6.
22. This is Frank Kermode's position as discussed by Paul Nelson in *Narrative and Morality: A Theological Inquiry* (University Park: Pennsylvania State University Press, 1987), p. 100.

metaphysical context within which it lived, gave a history of the sacred foundation of its social rituals, and provided concrete models of authentic life. Membership in the tribe involved retelling and acting out the shared stories which had been passed on from generation to generation since the beginning of time.[23]

According to Keen, "story" refers to a "metaphysical myth" that provides "the context for human identity."[24]

Such claims for story become clearer when contrasted with the claim that there is no such story or narrative which gives meaning to life. Keen refers to Jean-Paul Sartre's denial of such a "metaphysical myth" in his novel *Nausea:*

> This is what fools people: a man is always a teller of tales, he lives surrounded by his stories and the stories of others, he sees everything that happens to him through them; and he tries to live his own life as if he were telling a story.

> In real life there are no beginnings or endings; there are no moments of intrinsic significance which form a framework of meaning around experience. There are only days "tacked on to days without rhyme or reason, an interminable, monotonous addition."[25]

In Sartre's view, according to Keen, "no universal reason sets limits to the possible and gives meaning to human history."[26]

Ted Estess describes an entire movement in literature led by Samuel Beckett, who is probably best known as the author of the play *Waiting for Godot.* This movement denies the existence of a coherent story that gives meaning to human identity.[27] In making

23. Keen, *To a Dancing God.*
24. Ibid., p. 94.
25. Quoted by Keen in *To a Dancing God,* p. 95.
26. Keen, *To a Dancing God,* p. 95.
27. Estess describes contemporary literary artists who "speak of the death of the novel and despair over the story-form itself." These artists revel in the "immediate, the aleatory, and the unstructured." In addition to Beckett, Estess cites John Barth, Donald Barthelme, Ronald Sukenick,

his point, Estess quotes one of Beckett's narrators in *Stories and Texts for Nothing,* who claims that in making one's way through life's chaos, one has "no need of a story, a story is not compulsory, just a life." The narrator goes on to say, "That's the mistake I made, one of the mistakes, to have wanted a story for myself, whereas life alone is enough." The characters in Beckett's plays have no stories that give purpose to their movements. "Beckett's protagonists," Estess tells us, "typically depart with uncertain intentions, journey aimlessly, and seldom return." Beckett's characters have never found any meaningful order to life. They live outside any coherent story in a world of chaos, confusion, and aimless movement and thought. Life for them is "ill-heard" and "ill-murmured."[28]

In contrast to Sartre and Beckett, both Keen and Lehmann believe that there *are* stories that set "limits to the possible and give meaning to human history." Their judgments of which stories provide such limits and meaning, however, are different. Keen believes that the stories which give meaning to human existence must revolve around the *self* — that is, must take the form of individual biography.[29] Lehmann, on the other hand, believes that these stories must point to the transcendent — that is, must consist of stories about God's action. Keen and Lehmann represent two opposing directions taken by those who employ "story" in the development of theology. One begins with the narrative quality of human existence; the other begins with the narrative quality of God's action. We will examine each of these approaches before turn-

---

Earl Rauch, and Rudolph Wurlitzer as writers whose work reflects the "crises of story in recent literature" ("The Inenarrable Contraption: Reflections on the Metaphor of Story," *Journal of the American Academy of Religion* 42, no. 3 [Sept. 1974]: 415-34).

28. Estess, "The Inenarrable Contraption," pp. 417, 419, 423.

29. In searching for a story that gives meaning to life, Keen asserts that "no form of neo-orthodoxy provides a viable starting point. . . . Our starting point must be individual biography and history. If I am to discover the holy, it must be in *my* biography and not in the history of Israel. If there is a principle which gives unity and meaning to history, it must be something I touch, feel, and experience" (*To a Dancing God,* p. 99). On this point Keen's position could not be further from Lehmann's.

ing to the specific way in which Lehmann defines the concept of "story" for theological ethics.

The Narrative Character of Human Existence. Stephen Crites's article entitled "The Narrative Quality of Experience" has become the landmark article regarding the essentially narrative character of human experience.[30] Relying on Augustine, Crites says that humanity can "remember the past," "attend to the present," and "anticipate the future" because the temporal modalities of past, present, and future are located in the human memory itself — that is, memory preserves the images of things that have happened in the past with some sense of the order in which the events occurred.[31] In other words, events are stored in the memory in narrative form. Furthermore, the mind can "re-collect" these images and rearrange them to suit the purposes for which it calls them forth from memory.[32] The mind does this by telling stories. Stories neither destroy nor duplicate the narrative account stored in memory. They do, however, rearrange and reinterpret the events as new experiences are brought to the memory.[33]

Crites says that both sacred and mundane stories are used to re-collect memories. Sacred stories form the consciousness and identity of a people. These stories cannot be directly told but are expressed instead in ritual and dance, forming a "civili-

30. Crites, "The Narrative Quality of Experience," *Journal of the American Academy of Religion* 39 (September 1971): 291-311. This article has been reprinted in *Why Narrative?*, pp. 65-88.

31. Ibid., p. 298. If narrative is understood in its most basic form as giving an account of a sequence of events — past, present, and future — then human consciousness, Crites argues, has a narrative quality, for without the "temporal modalities" of past, present, and future, humanity would have only the momentary, disconnected experiences of the present. Humanity would then have no history and hence could not exist as humanity.

32. Story, therefore, is not only a form imposed upon remembered events in the process of recollection and expression; remembered events already have a narrative form preserved in the memory. Images are not stored in our minds as "atomic units." They are set in our minds in a certain sequence.

33. Crites, "The Narrative Quality of Experience," p. 301.

zation's sense of itself and of its world."[34] Mundane stories, on the other hand, are the stories that *can* be directly told, taking particular literary form such as legend, Scripture, and so on. It is the human consciousness with its incipient narrative capacity that mediates between the sacred and the mundane stories.[35]

Accepting Crites's proposition, some theologians claim that stories about the religious experience of an individual or group should form a central category for Christian theology. For instance, in the book *Diving Deep and Surfacing,* Carol Christ (pronounced "Crist"), in reaction to the male-oriented theology of her Christian training, turns to women's accounts of religious experience. Agreeing with Crites on the importance of story for the identity of the self, she sets out to show that women must begin to tell their own stories.[36]

Through the stories women tell about themselves, Carol Christ says, they come to recognize the boundaries of their identities and thereby acquire a sense of belonging in the world.

34. Ibid., p. 295.

35. Apparently Crites believes that a story is no longer sacred once it takes on verbal or written form. His definition of sacred includes the idea that the story cannot be directly told. One cannot help but notice the similarity between the pattern of human experience Crites establishes and Schleiermacher's description of the religious self-consciousness. According to Schleiermacher, religious language first emerges not in music or ritual, as Crites suggests, but as religious emotion in facial expressions or certain gestures. Eventually that emotion will be expressed in language, including the language of preaching and doctrine. While Crites does not describe the progress of religious language in this manner, he does, like Schleiermacher, distinguish between indirect expression of the sacred story in music and dance and the more direct speech of mundane stories that continue to express the original sacred story. Although Crites sets out to talk about narrative and Schleiermacher about the religious self-consciousness, they end up taking very similar positions. All that would be needed for deeper congruency would be for Crites to claim that one locates divine revelation in the narrative character of human existence and for Schleiermacher to assign a narrative character to the religious self-consciousness. See Schleiermacher, *The Christian Faith,* trans. H. R. Mackintosh and J. S. Stewart (Philadelphia: Fortress Press, 1976), p. 77.

36. Christ, *Diving Deep and Surfacing: Women Writers on Spiritual Quest* (Boston: Beacon Press, 1980), p. 4.

The stories they tell help them recognize and name the "great powers" or "the source of being." Telling their own stories and listening to each other's stories lead to a "mystical identification" that orients them to these great powers, to the world, and to other selves.[37] Neither the biblical story nor the notion of the "actions of God" plays a role in Carol Christ's book. According to her, God is not a personal agent who requires a story in order to be known. Rather, the self needs to share personal stories in order to experience an as yet unnamed god.

Sam Keen also believes that the narrative quality of human experience provides the only means by which to talk about religion. Biblical stories play no part in his theology, just as they play no part in Carol Christ's theology. In fact, besides Carol Christ's reference to "the great powers," there is little mention of God in the works by Keen and other like-minded writers. Stories about the self that lead to a sense of wholeness, a sense of identity, are called "sacred stories."[38] The claim that "God acts" is not necessary here. Sacred stories have to do with the self, not with God, although they can refer to a "higher power." It is, however, a power without a name, a power waiting to be named.

The Narrative Character of Revelation. For some theologians it is not the narrative quality of human experience that leads theology to employ the concept of story but the narrative quality of Scripture and divine revelation that dictates its use. According to Stanley Hauerwas, who belongs to this group, "We are 'storied people' because the God that sustains us is a 'storied God.'"[39] As Hauerwas explains,

> Like the self, God is a particular agent that can be known only as we know his story. Too often it has been assumed that we

37. Ibid., p. 13.
38. Clearly Sam Keen and Carol Christ define "sacred story" somewhat differently than Stephen Crites does.
39. Hauerwas, "The Church in a Divided World: The Interpretative Power of the Christian Story," in *A Community of Character: Toward a Constructive Christian Social Ethic* (Notre Dame: University of Notre Dame Press, 1981), p. 91.

can talk of God as if he is a universal, namely, that the grammar of God is like the grammar of trees, towns or persons. But the grammar of God is not that of an indefinite noun, but rather of a proper name. This means God is not a necessary being. God is not a concept, but a name.[40] In other words, the God of the Bible is a personal God who has a story.

Biblical narrative, therefore, presents God to us through stories.[41] Theologians who accept the narrative quality of divine revelation tend to interpret Scripture as presenting a picture of reality that calls us into its world. Accordingly, they reverse Gilkey's question regarding how we adjust the Bible to "fit" our modern worldview. The question becomes instead how we "fit" ourselves into the reality described by the Bible. "It is finally the narratives of Scripture that interpret us, not we who interpret the narratives," David Gouwens points out.[42] Thus the narrative quality of divine existence and biblical revelation informs the identity of the community that reads the biblical stories as canon.

The stories from the Bible provide the "primary data" or "raw material" for theological reflection.[43] These are in constant conversation with the story or history of the Christian community, which in turn tells stories to proclaim what it believes. Narrative becomes, in Hauerwas's phrase, the "primary grammar" of the Christian faith, because stories of God's action on

40. Hauerwas, "Story and Theology," in *Truthfulness and Tragedy: Further Investigations in Christian Ethics* (Notre Dame: University of Notre Dame Press, 1977), p. 79. In a similar fashion H. Richard Niebuhr points out that "the God of idealism generates principles, rules, formal attributes, but not a story" (*The Meaning of Revelation* [London: Macmillan, 1941], p. 35).

41. According to David Kelsey, God is known "directly in and with the story, and recedes from cognitive grasp the more he is abstracted from the story" (Kelsey, *The Uses of Scripture in Recent Theology* [Philadelphia: Fortress Press, 1975], p. 39).

42. Gouwens, "Is There Theology after Karl Barth?" unpublished manuscript, p. 5.

43. Stroup, *The Promise of Narrative Theology*, p. 17.

our behalf provide the source of Christian identity.[44] Our understanding of who we are, what we believe, and what we are to do arises from the stories that have been passed down from generation to generation.

Theologians who employ "story" based on claims for the narrative character of divine revelation do not replace analysis of Christian doctrine with the telling of stories. Rather, they make a distinction between primary and secondary religious language. Primary religious language is the language of faith being spoken in worship, in prayer, and in confession. It is the language of witness. The tendency to "tell the old, old story" is one form of primary (or first-order) religious discourse. The discipline of systematic theology, on the other hand, is called "secondary discourse." It analyzes the church's primary speech about God, and it reflects on that speech by formulating and interpreting doctrine. Here the language is more technical, because it is primarily the language of analytical reflection, not the language typically used in worship, in prayer, or in confession. The tasks of systematic theology are to reflect on and analyze the story *of* the faith and to reflect on what the concept of story means *for* the faith. Both of these activities are removed from actual story-telling.

How These Stories Are True. Using story as a theological category raises the question of standards for measuring truth. The danger that story poses for theological ethics lies in the indifference to moral judgment that arises when one is compelled to say, "You tell your story, and I'll tell mine; as long as we are true to ourselves, no one can say we are wrong." George Lindbeck's recent book entitled *The Nature of Doctrine* describes three theories of religion, each offering a different explanation for the truth of religious claims.[45] These theories can add insight into the different reasons why theological approaches employ or reject the concept of story.

44. Hauerwas, *Peaceable Kingdom* (Notre Dame: University of Notre Dame Press, 1983), pp. 24-25.
45. Lindbeck, *The Nature of Doctrine: Religion and Theology in a Post-liberal Age* (Philadelphia: Westminster Press, 1984).

(1) The Cognitive-Propositional Theory. The first theory says that Christian doctrines are propositional statements of truth — that is, the Christian faith makes absolute, unchanging claims to truth. Lindbeck calls this point of view the "cognitive-propositional" approach and assigns its use to the "preliberals." Those who adhere to this position shy away from the concept of "story" altogether, suspicious of its association with "myth" and "fairy tale." This is the stance Langdon Gilkey attacks because of its literal interpretation of the claim that "God acts."

(2) The Experiential-Expressive Theory. The second theory interprets doctrine as expressions of religious experience. This position rests on the assumption that religious experience is universal. Although different traditions describe religious experience in different ways, they finally are all saying essentially the same thing. Lindbeck calls this the "experiential-expressive" approach, which is most often used by the theological tradition of liberalism.

This position is consistent with that held by those who, like Carol Christ and Sam Keen, rely on the anthropological interpretation of narrative — that is, on the assumption that human experience is essentially and universally narrative, and that from it religious narrative is bound to spring. The truth of religion is associated with its "symbolic efficacy" — that is, truth is measured by how well religious symbols express the inner religious experience common to humankind. While theologians in this group can readily employ story as a theological category, religious stories are not "necessarily about the gods," as Crites says. In experiential-expressive theory, claims for God's actions tend to be set aside, with emphases placed on human experience and expression, on the stories that spring from within us.

(3) The Cultural-Linguistic Theory. Lindbeck's third theory describes doctrines not as truth claims or as descriptions of religious experience but as "regulative rules" of faith. Religion is akin to linguistic and cultural structures that are not composed of propositional statements of truth but are the media in which one lives. (In other words, doctrines serve as regulative rules of faith

within the media or ethos established by religion.) This "cultural-linguistic" interpretation of religion reverses the relationship between inner religious experience and outward expression presented by the expressivist view. Religion is not derived from inner experience; inner experience is formed by religion. As Lindbeck explains, "the objectivities" of religion come first — that is, "its language, doctrines, liturgies, and modes of action." These "objectivities" subsequently shape human passions into religious experiences.[46] Lindbeck assigns the cultural-linguistic interpretation to the "postliberal movement."

According to this view, the structure provided by religion is often expressed in the form of story. As Lindbeck explains, "Religions are seen as comprehensive interpretive schemes, usually embodied in myths or narratives and heavily ritualized, which structure human experience and understanding of self and world." Lindbeck explains that not every story is a religious story. Only those stories that organize the beliefs and actions of the listeners in relation to that which has ultimate significance for them are religious stories.[47]

The linguistic approach is vulnerable to the charge that it interprets structure itself as reality, thus leading to the most extreme form of relativism — that is, every story is true if the different parts are consistent with one another. In other words, it leads to what Lindbeck calls "intrasystematic truth."

---

46. Ibid., p. 39. This reversal of the inner and outer aspects of religion allows Lindbeck to refute the idea that all religions are simply expressions of the same universal religious experience. Different religions made up of different stories, myths, and doctrines can produce vastly different religious experiences, as he explains: "A Balinese, molded by a ceremonial system in which is embedded a partly Hindu and partly animist world view, will fall into a catatonic trance when confronted by types of stimulus that might plunge a Westerner, influenced by a long tradition of biblical monotheism, into strenuous activity." Therefore, according to Lindbeck, "it seems implausible to claim that religions are diverse objectifications of the same basic experience" (ibid., pp. 40-41). See also Richard John Neuhaus, "Is There Theological Life after Liberalism? The Lindbeck Proposal," *Dialogue* 24 (Winter 1985): 66.

47. Lindbeck, *The Nature of Doctrine*, pp. 32-33.

Nevertheless, intrasystematic truth remains an essential indicator of truth. In fact, Lindbeck says that a religion, along with the stories and doctrines it generates, must include intrasystematic truth in order to make any claim to truth at all. For instance, the claim "Christ is Lord" is intrasystematically true when consistent with other Christian claims *and* with Christian patterns of action. Thus, in the latter instance, persecuting a nonbeliever in the name of the lordship of Christ constitutes a denial of the truth, because it is inconsistent with the Christian affirmation that lordship points to the suffering servant.[48]

Intrasystematic truth is both practical and logical. It is practical because it says the truth of a religion cannot be divorced from the behavior it produces, and it is logical because it measures the consistency of doctrines — that is, whether the claim of one doctrine contradicts the claims of others. Intrasystematic truth alone, however, is an inadequate indicator of a second type of truth important to the linguistic approach: ontological truth. Whereas intrasystematic truth points to the coherence or consistency of claims, ontological truth points to the correspondence between those claims and reality.

Lindbeck knows that to ignore ontological truth altogether lands one in a radically relativistic position which he wants to avoid. The cultural-linguistic position, he says, affirms the ontological truth of religious claims when propositional and "performative" statements are joined together. In other words, a religious claim corresponds to the truth "only insofar as it is a performance, an act or deed which helps create that correspondence."[49] As an example, Lindbeck refers to Paul's and Luther's claims for the lordship of Christ:

> Paul and Luther . . . quite clearly believed that Christ's Lordship is objectively real no matter what the faith or unfaith of

---

48. Ibid., p. 64.

49. Ibid. Lindbeck is here relying on the work of J. L. Austin. In addition, see Christopher L. Morse, *The Logic of Promise in Moltmann's Theology* (Philadelphia: Fortress Press, 1979).

those who hear or say the words. What they [claimed] is that the only way to assert this truth is to do something about it, i.e., to commit oneself to a way of life; and this concern, it would seem, is wholly congruent with the suggestion that it is only through the performatory use of religious utterances that they acquire propositional force.[50]

In another example, Lindbeck says that to claim that Jesus was raised from the dead warrants "behaving in the ways recommended by the resurrection stories even when one grants the impossibility of specifying the mode in which these stories signify."[51]

Lindbeck also claims that truth can be measured only in the context in which it is stated. To illustrate his point, he uses the statement "The car is red." One does not know if that statement is true or false unless one knows to which particular car it refers. The same is true of religious language. One must be "inside the relevant context" to assess its truth. "This means," says Lindbeck, "that one must have some skill in how to use its language and practice its way of life before the propositional meaning of its affirmations becomes determinate enough to be rejected."[52] In other words, those who do not know the language of the faith cannot affirm the truth of the claim that "Christ is Lord," but neither can they deny it. The claim does convey ontological truth, but only as the believer participates in the claim by undertaking activities that help mold the believer's mind to the mind of Christ — for example, worship, promise-hearing and promise-keeping, obedience, and so on. In the cultural-linguistic approach, doctrines serve not as propositional statements of truth but as second-order discourse that reflects on and regulates the primary discourse of believers, who do make ontological claims for truth.[53]

Many critics rightly claim that Lindbeck falls short of demonstrating the ontological truth of religious claims. How, for instance, by using Lindbeck's approach does one disprove the truth

50. Ibid., p. 66.
51. Ibid., p. 67.
52. Ibid., p. 68.
53. Ibid., p. 69.

of the Nazi story and its claims for the superiority of the Arian race, or the story of American slave-owners in the nineteenth century? If one can prove that these stories were intrasystematically true and that they produced behavior consistent with their claims, how can one disprove their ontological efficacy?

Despite the deficiencies of Lindbeck's approach, the major aspects of his cultural-linguistic interpretation of Christianity coincide with the theology of those who set out to show not only the narrative character of human existence but also the narrative character of revelation, biblical witness, and, indeed, every aspect of the Christian religion. Lehmann's work falls under this category.

Lehmann's Position

Lehmann's understanding of the necessity of "story" for theology includes both the idea of the narrative quality of divine revelation and the need for narrative in human existence. A "saving" story, he says, arises when God's story and the human story are in "conversation" with each other.

Story as Metaphor. Lehmann says "story" refers to any account of human origin, development, and destiny. His work indicates that the Christian faith is "story-shaped" because it gives an account of human life from "origin to destiny, from beginnings to consummating endings."[54] He defines story as "the narration in the power of language and of social cohesion of what it takes to be and to stay human in the world."[55] Thus "story" brings us again to his theme of humanization. He makes a distinction, however, between "story" and "saving story" based on the relationship between humanization and transcendence.

---

54. Lehmann, "The Indian Situation as a Question of Accountability," *Church and Society,* January/February 1985, p. 61. The term "story-shaped" is from an unpublished essay by David Gouwens entitled "Is There Theology after Karl Barth?"

55. Lehmann, *The Transfiguration of Politics* (New York: Harper & Row, 1975), p. 10.

While "story" refers to any narrative account of what is required for humanization to occur, a "saving story" recognizes that humanization requires transcendence. In addition, the "saving story" itself provides the avenue through which we experience that transcendence. A "saving story," therefore, "is the mode of the experience of a presence in the present whose power liberates as it binds and binds as it liberates."[56] Thus "story" brings us back to the concept of the politics of God.

Lehmann claims that descriptions of humanization and the politics of God take on narrative form for three reasons: (1) because talk about revelation as recorded in Scripture requires making reference to the concept of story, (2) because talk about human beings and their identities and actions requires making reference to the concept of story, and (3) because it is in the conversation between the divine and the human stories that a "saving story" emerges. It will be helpful to deal with each of these assertions in turn.

(1) The Narrative Quality of Divine Revelation and Scripture. According to Lehmann, "one cannot think as a Christian without presupposing a certain way of understanding the Bible":

> The reality and activity of God, the shaping of a community of faith in consequence of the divine activity, the apprehension of the divine activity and the historical life and destiny of the community of faith — all are involved in the simple act of taking up the Bible to read. To ignore these considerations is to ignore the crucial question of the possibility and validity of theological knowledge.[57]

Lehmann identifies two dangers that threaten our understanding of the Bible as revelation. One danger lies in imposing our own ideas on the text with no regard for what the biblical writer intended, the other in overemphasizing the original setting of the text so that its meaning as revelation for today is

---

56. Ibid.
57. Lehmann, *Ethics in a Christian Context* (New York: Harper & Row, 1963), p. 26.

lost.[58] Both approaches challenge the credibility of the Bible as revelation, one by making the interpretation of revelation vulnerable to human whimsy, the other by confining revelation to the past. Lehmann believes that to avoid these dangers one must examine the complex relation between faith and the Bible with a carefully formulated hermeneutic. He has been criticized for not delivering what he insists is necessary, yet in reading his work one finds that the idea of story clearly supplies him with a primary hermeneutical principle.

Lehmann recognizes that not all biblical material takes narrative form. In addition to the stories of the Old and New Testaments there are also the Commandments, wisdom sayings, psalms, epistles, and so on.[59] He contends, however, that these non-narrative portions of the Bible are unintelligible if read apart from their narrative context. For example, the Decalogue read as an independent list of "Thou shalts" and "Thou shalt nots" is not the same as the Decalogue read in the context of the story of the Hebrews' liberation from Egypt, their wanderings in the desert, their disobedience, and their covenantal relation with God. Only in the context of this narrative do we rightly interpret the Decalogue.

---

58. Yarbro Collins describes the same two dangers of biblical interpretation in *Crisis and Catharsis: The Power of the Apocalypse* (Philadelphia: Westminster Press, 1984). The first danger is that of interpreting everything in the Bible as having to do primarily with our own time. This interpretation claims that the Bible is filled with predictions that apply to our time more accurately than to the time of the biblical writers. This is the error of fundamentalist literalism and neo-apocalypticism. At a far more sophisticated level it is the danger of pure literary or structural analysis.

The second danger arose primarily with the development of the historical-critical method in the nineteenth century. This method examines in detail the context of the text. It asks who the writer was, where the text was written, what language it was written in, and who the intended audience was, including the audience's political and social milieu. The danger of overemphasizing what the text meant in its own context, however, is that it becomes irrelevant as anything but a historical document. We are no longer susceptible to being grasped by the dynamic nature of its truth. We study it for what it tells us about how things were; we do not really learn much about ourselves or how things are today.

59. Lehmann, *Ethics in a Christian Context*, p. 77.

The concept of story, therefore, serves the Reformed principle that Scripture interprets Scripture — that is, that one arrives at the meaning of a passage from Scripture by interpreting it in light of the whole biblical narrative. Each individual passage is understood only in the context of the biblical story of God's movement on behalf of the world through creation, redemption, and promised destiny.

From the biblical narrative, Lehmann says, we discover certain images describing God and God's ways with humanity. In turning to these images, however, Lehmann recalls Abraham Heschel's caution against "imaging" God. Heschel warned against the danger "of giving primacy to concepts and dogmas" about God, which are only "reminders" of God. According to Heschel, "wonder and radical amazement" — not concepts, descriptions, or images — are the avenues to God: "However subtle and noble our concepts may be, as soon as they become descriptive, namely, definite, they confine Him [God] and force Him into the triteness of our minds. . . . To form an image of Him or His acts is to deny His existence."[60]

Lehmann believes that Heschel's strict warning against this form of idolatry is in keeping with the Old Testament admonition against graven images. He also believes, however, that both the Old and New Testaments give the human imagination some leeway in its search to find appropriate images for describing God. That Scripture usually reveals God's self through the spoken word coupled with the biblical use of "word pictures" (parables) causes Lehmann to believe that "the Bible makes room for another dimension of the imagination than mere fancy or idolatry."[61] This dimension lies in the parabolic images that are found and interpreted in light of the biblical narrative as a whole.

It is in the parabolic images of the Old and New Testaments that Lehmann finds the connection between revelation and im-

---

60. Lehmann, *Ethics in a Christian Context,* pp. 86ff. Lehmann is referring to Heschel's book entitled *God in Search of Man* (New York: Farrar, Straus, & Cudahy, 1955), pp. 345-55, 187.

61. Ibid., p. 88.

agination as well as the grounds for talking about the activity of God. He believes that the "parabolic image" can juxtapose God's ways and human ways without confusing or separating them.[62] Parabolic images, Lehmann argues, free the reader's biblical imagination from confinement to the text — that is, they free the biblical interpreter from a literalistic interpretation of Scripture. In describing the activity of God, parabolic images can "leave" the pages of the text and be employed in the "literary and historical context" outside the Bible.

Lehmann's position is here consistent with Barth's claim that we do not interpret the Bible so much as the Bible interprets us.[63] Like Barth before him, Lehmann says that rather than "de-mythologizing" the Bible in order to discover its meaning for today, we need to have the Bible "mythologize" our present situation so that we can properly interpret it. In other words, we do not need to force an interpretation on the Bible to make it contemporaneous with us; we need instead to put our situation in line with the Bible.

(2) The Need for Narrative in Human Existence. This leads to the second reason Lehmann believes that Christian theology demands attention to story: the affirmation that talk about human identity requires narrative. Lehmann does not make this claim based on a notion of an essentially narrative quality of human nature or experience, as Crites does, but makes this assertion because humanization requires the presence of the transcendence of which story gives an account.

For Lehmann, the primary task of ethics is to discern those forces that break human society apart and to examine what is required to keep human society together in humanizing freedom and order. He describes an attitude, atmosphere, or ethos that promotes human community. That ethos, he says, is created by the action of God in Jesus Christ (the presence of transcendence), which is described in Scripture and handed down in the

---

62. Ibid., p. 90.
63. Barth, "Strange New World of the Bible," in *Word of God, Word of Man* (Gloucester, Mass.: Peter Smith, 1978).

tradition of the *koinonia*. Theological ethics describes God's action on our behalf and hence gives us a vision of the world as a gift of God's acts of creation and redemption.

Like Stanley Hauerwas, Lehmann believes we act responsibly only when we are trained to "envision the world."[64] A "saving story" provides the vision to see the world in a way that promotes humanization:

> A story that saves is a story that offers insight and language, and through these a power of symbolization and structuralization through which the tension, and ultimately the conflict, between gratitude and power in social interaction are overcome in a social order that is instrumental to the freedom that being human takes.[65]

The narrative account of God's grace on behalf of humanity gives Christians the proper vision to "see" the world truthfully. Through that description we come to understand our vocation in the world — that is, who we are called to be and what we are called responsibly to do. Accordingly, a saving story gives the insight we need to develop the symbols and the structure that create a human order that promotes human freedom.[66]

(3) Conversation between God's Story and the Human Story. Lehmann employs the concept of "story" because he recognizes

---

64. On this point both Lehmann and Hauerwas are in line with Calvin, who says that Scripture provides the necessary "spectacles" through which we can properly see the world (*Institutes of the Christian Religion*, I.4).

65. Lehmann, *The Transfiguration of Politics*, p. 248.

66. Ibid., p. 248. The biblical narrative from creation to destiny defines who we are. The parabolic images from the Bible inform the vision we have of our own situation. Hauerwas agrees with Lehmann on this point: "We neither are nor should we be formed primarily by the publicly defensible rules we hold, but by the stories and metaphors through which we learn to intend the variety of our existence. Metaphors and stories suggest how we should see and describe the world — that is, how we should 'look on' ourselves, others, and the world — in a way that rules taken in themselves do not. Stories and metaphors do this by providing the narrative accounts that give our lives coherence" (*Vision and Virtue: Essays in Ethical Reflection* [Notre Dame: University of Notre Dame Press, 1974], p. 71).

that the Christian faith is "story-shaped" — that is, it gives a narrative account of human origins, development, and destiny. It is a saving story because it gives an account of God's participation in human identity. Lehmann does not, however, replace theological analysis or Christian doctrine with the telling of stories.[67] Like other theologians, he makes an implicit distinction between primary and secondary language. Stories belong to the primary expression of the faith; theology, as the secondary expression of the faith, reflects on those stories:

> Theology, as an activity of thinking and interpretation, is properly understood and practiced as a reflection upon the constitutive story of what has been discovered and believed about the ultimate and the ongoing experience of the world as the environment of life as human life. . . . The word, 'theology,' refers to thinking about God in the context of the story which the experience of God evokes, and of what, in consequence, that story has to tell.[68]

The primary source for what Lehmann calls "saving" stories is neither the narrative of human experience nor the biblical narrative alone. Rather, the saving story through which Christians

---

67. Lehmann's theological ethics is not informed by religious biography or autobiography. He rarely sets out to give an account of the individual lives of the faithful. He makes autobiographical references even less frequently. While he is interested in biographical works such as Bethge's biography of Dietrich Bonhoeffer, Busch's book on Karl Barth, and Fox's recent account of the life of Reinhold Niebuhr, he does not use biography as a category for theological ethics. Nevertheless, in lectures Lehmann has given accounts of his impressions of these personal histories. He seems to view these pieces as somewhat self-indulgent, although he does take pleasure in them. It is clear that Lehmann personally views the telling of stories as a significant part of handing on the tradition of faith from one generation to the next. It is unlikely, however, that he wants to elevate biographical sketches to a formal category for the discipline of theology. One does not "do" theological ethics by telling stories about theologians, although such stories may indeed prompt theological and ethical thought and action. Telling stories can never take the place of careful theological analysis of Christian doctrines and their relationship to Christian life.

68. Lehmann, "Identity, Difference and Human Community," p. 22.

experience the transcendent arises from the "conversation" that occurs between the biblical narrative and the human situation.[69] The biblical text, the church's confessions, the history of the tradition, and the present situation must be interpreted in a dynamic relationship, as Lehmann explains: "There is a kind of reciprocal clarification going on. The text illuminates in a particular way certain attempts to understand the situation and the situation brings somehow fresh vitality and enlargement of the horizon to the text which one never really knew before."[70] At the heart of Lehmann's ethic lies the running conversation between the biblical texts and the human situation.

Lehmann holds that the "transcendence" revealed by the biblical narrative and parabolic images refers, above all else, to Jesus of Nazareth. Jesus is "the revelation of God in and through whom all other apprehensions of God's activity are to be criticized and comprehended."[71] Nevertheless, the revelation of Jesus the Messiah found in the biblical narrative is not rightly and completely known until it is placed in conversation with the human situation. Lehmann points out that in his career as a theologian he has focused on giving an account of that running conversation.[72]

Lehmann does not always draw a sharp line between primary and secondary language. His understanding that parable serves both biblical interpretation and interpretation of the world leads him to turn readily to the language of poetry. Believ-

---

69. Marvin Brown, "A Conversation with Paul Lehmann on Biblical Hermeneutics," unpublished interview. One of Lehmann's principles for biblical hermeneutics is this: "There is always a running conversation between the Bible and the contemporary situation, and thus any attempt to probe the human situation with any range and depth involves an interaction between the Bible and that situation" (p. 1).

70. According to Lehmann, "This is what the Reformers meant by the *testimonium internum spiritus sancti* ("A Conversation with Paul Lehmann on Biblical Hermeneutics").

71. Lehmann, *Ethics in a Christian Context,* p. 89. For this reason Lehmann agrees with the Reformers that the content and the authority of the Bible are the same — that is, Jesus Christ is both the content and the authority.

72. Brown, "A Conversation with Paul Lehmann on Biblical Hermeneutics."

ing that humanization and the politics of God are as much a matter of the heart as the head, Lehmann asserts that the language of story and poetry, rather than the language of metaphysics, describes the concern of ethics:

> Ultimately ethics is more akin to art than to metaphysics. For the price which metaphysics pays for its admirable clarification and ordering of the conceptual description of the nature of reality, or virtue, or obligation, is loss of sensitivity to what is concretely and fundamentally human. Art, on the other hand, is the province of sensitivity both to nature and to man where what is concretely and fundamentally human is continually taking shape and being reshaped.[73]

Lehmann believes that humanization requires imagination more than logic, images more than concepts.[74] This does not mean that he replaces rigorous theological analysis with poetry any more than he replaces theology with storytelling. He does, however, believe that human imagination is required to relate God's revelation in Christ as recorded in the Bible to our present situation.

This helps explain why Lehmann's writing is sometimes devoid of the concrete definitions that some readers seek and is instead replete with frequent references to poetry, attempts to discover metaphorical connections between the etymological meaning of words and their everyday use, and plays on words that go beyond literal meanings.

For Lehmann, the relation between revelation and imagination is always defined primarily and essentially by the parabolic images — usually political ones — used by Jesus to describe God. According to Lehmann, therefore, God is not *defined* but *described* by theology's use of parabolic images. Because story is indispensable for describing the Christian faith, and because theology

---

73. Lehmann, "Integrity of Heart," in *Ecumenical Dialogue at Harvard: The Roman Catholic–Protestant Colloquium,* ed. Samuel H. Miller and G. Ernest Wright (Cambridge: Harvard University Press, 1964), p. 279.
74. Lehmann, *Ethics in a Christian Context,* p. 86.

has a descriptive task, theology cannot ignore the language of story, even though it does not itself have to tell stories.

Lehmann hopes his ethics will accomplish two objectives in its focus on the narrative form required by humanization and the politics of God. First, he hopes to teach his readers how to read the Bible properly. We live in a time, he says, that has forgotten how to read between the lines.[75] For instance, contemporary readers of the Bible who find the texts sexist are resorting to as literalistic a reading as any Christian fundamentalist. Alternatively, Lehmann relies on the Reformed principle that Scripture interprets Scripture. We should not read each individual text, pericope, or story in isolation, he says. We should read each text in light of the whole narrative, and employ all of the biblical images in our interpretation of one passage.

Second, Lehmann, through his repeated recourse to biblical and poetic images, wants to teach his readers to read the signs of the times. He does not promote "intuitionism," as some of his critics claim.[76] He does, however, want to cultivate what he calls the "biblical imagination" by putting the Bible in constant conversation with the present situation. The biblical images can interpret our situation just as our situation brings its interpretation to the Bible.

Lehmann wants to teach us to read both the Bible and the signs of the times. His ethics seeks to identify those images from the Bible that are in conversation with the present situation and thus create the ethos required for humanization to occur. In his theological ethics, the human situation, pathos, and responsibility are always in the forefront. Lehmann will not interpret the Bible independently of the human situation, nor talk about the human situation independently of the Bible. His work begins at the juncture where the two are in conversation. When humanization occurs as a result of that conversation, one can say *there* is an act of God.

75. Lehmann, wedding sermon preached at First Presbyterian Church, Jacksonville, Texas, 13 Apr. 1985.
76. Nelson, *Narrative and Morality*, p. 94.

The Truth of Christian Stories. If the stories and images of the Bible are not literal references to God's speaking audibly or eyewitness accounts of divine acts, Langdon Gilkey asks, how can they inform what we mean today when we say "God acts"? Since many of the biblical stories are not history but myth, written by storytellers, how can they contain divine revelation that interprets our world and what we are to do today?

Lehmann never sets out to answer these questions. Consistent with his entire methodology, he never attempts to *prove* the existence of God but to *describe* the action of God, whose existence is sure. He uses "story" as a category for describing what faith holds about the claim that "God acts," not as proof for faith. He consciously avoids the question of proof. Whereas the appeal to story prompts some to ask if these stories depend on belief in a transcendent God or *create* that transcendent God, Lehmann contends that neither the storyteller nor the faithful listener asks this question. Consistent with Lindbeck's "cultural-linguistic" position, Lehmann believes that theology works within the world of the story, which itself points to a power outside the story. Where did that knowledge come from prior to the telling of the first faithful story? Again, neither the storyteller nor the faithful listener is interested in that question. Lehmann stands boldly within the tradition of faith speaking to faith. He writes from a confessional standpoint that does not value so-called proofs for faith.[77]

Lehmann begins, as Calvin did, with the *assumption* that knowledge of God is a gift from God. Like Calvin, he does not set out to give an epistemological argument for God. He simply speaks of revelation, of knowing God's will, as if it made sense

---

77. With William James he can say, "What religion reports . . . always purports to be an act of experience; the divine is actually present, religion says, and between it and ourselves relations of give and take are actual. If definite perceptions of acts like this cannot stand upon their own feet, surely abstract reasoning cannot give them the support they are in need of." Lehmann does not, however, subscribe to James's understanding of "over-belief" (Lehmann, *Ethics in a Christian Context,* p. 196). For Lehmann's discussion of "over-belief," see *Ethics in a Christian Context,* p. 199.

to do so. The justification he offers for our ability to talk about God is that Scripture promises us that we can:[78]

> The Bible never defines God's nature but always describes his activity. The crucial point in the biblical description takes the form of an event in which God so exposed himself as to make it unmistakable what he was up to. He exposed himself in a great act of humanization which theology calls incarnation. Incarnation in the last analysis means the act of God's humanization whereby in the life, death and resurrection of Jesus of Nazareth, he signalled to all mankind what the score was in the world in which men were living in order to be human.[79]

The only measure of the truth of these stories lies in humanization.

The Bible, Lehmann says, tells us stories about a God who acts in certain ways. As people whose lives are formed by those narratives, we continue to see God's action in certain events. When human beings are transformed by the freedom to live in humanizing relationships, we say "God acts." Lehmann's position does require human imagination, as both his critics and his supporters point out. His is not, however, an ethic of intuitionism that "leaves everything to the eye of the beholder," as Paul Nelson claims.[80] The Bible gives us the primary images, which in turn are in constant conversation with the contemporary situation. We work out our

78. From a reading of Ephesians, Lehmann can claim, "There you have it! It is possible — in the world, here and now — to know what God is up to and has been doing since the world began. This knowledge is plain and open to all men, everywhere in the world, for this is exactly what Jesus Christ is all about. If we orient our lives to him we not only know God but are confidently in touch with God and have no doubt about what God's will is. God's will is that all men should grow into personal maturity in and through the experience of a community in which everyone is personally and trustworthily open to and concerned for everyone else as a person" (Lehmann, "The Transforming Power of the Church," *The Intercollegian,* Jan. 1954, p. 6).

79. Lehmann, "Environment of Authentic Selfhood," *The Intercollegian,* March 1959, p. 9.

80. Ibid.

understanding of God's will and action in conversation with the Bible, the Christian tradition, and one another in light of the significant facts of the situation in which we stand.

Story as a Theological Concept: A Warning. In his analysis of Samuel Beckett's "storyless" characters, Ted Estess claims that theologians who want to employ the concept of story need to pay attention to literature like Beckett's that "disrupts" the form of story. Estess believes that a theologian who reads Beckett is faced with two challenges in incorporating the concept of story into theology.

First, Estess challenges theologians not to use the category of story as a means to ignore the chaos of life that Beckett so powerfully describes:

> The use of story as a heuristic device to construe the meaning of existence has the danger of our substituting a syntactical order of necessity, either logical, causal, or teleological, for the surprising disorder of lived possibilities. Just as the wondering and curious response is heightened by the disruption of the story-form in Beckett's art, so may such a response to our own existence be enhanced if things are not coerced neatly into place in a well-shaped plot.[81]

As we seek to tell a story that gives order to the chaos, we must be careful not to allow that order to become a violent imposition. By way of an extreme example, one thinks of the "story" generated by Nazi Germany that gave Aryans an identity the hallmark of which was a sense of superiority to the rest of humanity, or of slave-owners in America whose story imposed an order on life that denied freedom to black men and women. Similarly, Lehmann speaks about the story of white Americans that allowed them to slaughter American Indians in the name of western advancement.[82]

The second challenge for theologians interested in story as

---

81. Estess, "The Inenarrable Contraption," pp. 431-32.
82. This is one of the points of Lehmann's essay entitled "The Indian Situation as a Question of Accountability."

a theological category involves the need to examine carefully the relation between life and literature. As Estess points out, "Beckett's disgust with storied literature reflects, in part, a recognition that life is considerably more mysterious and ambiguous than the form of story sometimes implies." While Estess admits that story provides one way to describe human life, he reminds us that it is only *one* way. In the words of Roland Barthes, Estess warns that story becomes a "death" if it "transforms life into destiny, a memory into a useful act, duration into an oriented and meaningful time."[83] Accordingly, theology can err if it uses story to give facile explanations for the mysteries of existence, especially those mysteries which have to do with human suffering. In other words, story can function in precisely the opposite way from that which Lehmann intends.

Lehmann's understanding of the apocalyptic character of divine revelation takes heed of these two dangers. It is to this concept that we now turn.

83. Estess, "The Inenarrable Contraption," pp. 432-33.

IV

The Significance of Apocalyptic
for Lehmann's Ethics

In the preceding three chapters I have described Paul Lehmann's approach to theological ethics by offering definitions of his primary terms and by comparing Lehmann's ethics to other contextual ethics. These emphases led to the critical question, "What does Lehmann mean when he claims 'God acts'?" To clarify Lehmann's claims regarding the action of God, I explored the concepts of revelation and narrative. In this present chapter I will expand the discussion of Lehmann's understanding of God's action by examining his use of the idea of apocalyptic.[1]

Like "story," the concept of apocalyptic at once informs the foundation of Lehmann's work and needs further clarification and development. Also like the concept of story, this concept is difficult to define. In light of the ambiguity of the term, one might wonder why anyone would set out to untangle Lehmann's complex ideas and imagery with an equally difficult concept! I

1. A portion of this chapter has been published as a separate essay. See Nancy J. Duff, "The Significance of Pauline Apocalyptic for Theological Ethics," in *Apocalyptic and the New Testament: Essays in Honor of J. Louis Martyn*, ed. Joel Marcus and Marion L. Soards, Journal for the Study of the New Testament Supplement Series, no. 24 (Sheffield Academic Press, 1989), pp. 279-96.

make the attempt because a striking similarity exists between emphases in Lehmann's work and claims made by New Testament scholars such as C. K. Bekker, Ernst Käsemann, and J. Louis Martyn regarding the apocalyptic character of the Pauline epistles. These similarities indicate that an examination of the research into Pauline apocalyptic could further elucidate Lehmann's method for theological ethics. In the following pages I will explore four characteristics of Pauline apocalyptic and the work of Paul Lehmann: (1) the understanding of revelation as radical discontinuity, (2) an emphasis on the Lordship of Christ, (3) the understanding that we are living at the turn of the ages, and (4) the expectation of an imminent parousia.

Revelation as Radical Discontinuity

According to the New Testament scholar J. Louis Martyn, an apocalypse is "an event that brings into existence something that was not there before."[2] Apocalyptic thought in the New Testament claims that through God's revelation in Jesus Christ, God changed the very structure of reality. Revelation, understood apocalyptically, *is* the transformation of the world. Revelation is the bringing into existence of that which was not there before.

"Revelation" is the English word most frequently used to translate the Greek word "apocalypse." According to Martyn, however, it provides only an inadequate translation.[3] "Apocalypse" does not only mean the unveiling of something already existing but heretofore unknown, as the word "revelation" often indicates. "Apocalypse" also means the "invasion" of God's grace into the world, an invasion that brings into existence that which was not there before. Romans 4:17, which refers to the God who "gives life to the dead and calls into existence the things that

2. Martyn, "Galatians 3:28, Faculty Appointments, and the Overcoming of Christological Amnesia," record of remarks made to UTS Alumni/ae in San Francisco on 21 Dec. 1981, p. 1.

3. Martyn, "From Paul to Flannery O'Connor," *Katallagete* 7.4 (Winter 1981): 11.

do not exist," becomes a key passage describing the apocalyptic understanding of revelation.[4]

Martyn, therefore, expands the very brief definition of apocalyptic given by Käsemann, who simply defines it as "expectation of an imminent parousia."[5] Martyn claims that while Paul did expect the end to come soon, he also believed that the turning of the ages *had already begun*. Paul believed that we do not live completely in the New Age but that the New Age (or New Creation) has, nevertheless, already been inaugurated in Jesus Christ. We live, therefore, at the juncture of the ages.[6]

From Martyn's description of Pauline apocalyptic, one can say that its primary characteristic is that it presents revelation as radically discontinuous with the present state of reality in the world. Apocalyptic thought believes that revelation never arises as a natural structure in the world but breaks in from beyond and stands in conflict with the present state of things.

This theme of radical discontinuity is not unique to Pauline apocalyptic. Jewish and Christian literary apocalypses also interpret divine revelation as standing in stark contrast to the structures of the world. Paul's description of revelation as radical discontinuity in relation to the world differs from that found in the apocalypses, however, because Paul interprets the cross as *the* apocalyptic event that has changed the world and our way of perceiving it. Thus, while revelation *is* the transformation of

---

4. See also 1 Corinthians 1:28-29.

5. Käsemann, "On the Subject of Primitive Christian Apocalyptic," in *New Testament Questions of Today* (Philadelphia: Fortress Press, 1969), p. 109.

6. Vincent Branick describes Paul's belief that the end time had begun: "Paul differs from traditional apocalyptic . . . in his faith that the end time has begun with the resurrection of Christ. Christ's resurrection for Paul is above all 'the first fruits' of the general resurrection (1 Cor. 15.20). The Spirit already given is the 'down payment' of eschatological blessings (2 Cor. 1.22). Paul's apocalyptic, therefore, exhibits the paradoxical tension of the 'already' and the 'not yet.' Existence according to the Spirit takes place fully only at the resurrection (1 Cor. 15.42-44), yet the resurrection of Christ has already taken place" (Branick, "Apocalyptic Paul?" *Catholic Biblical Quarterly* 47 [1985]: 666).

the world, one cannot understand any and every change in the world as divine apocalypse. One can interpret transformation of the world as divine revelation only when that transformation is consistent with God's action in the cross and resurrection of Jesus Christ.

In turning to Lehmann's work, one discovers this same emphasis on divine revelation as radically discontinuous with present reality. Lehmann implicitly agrees with Jürgen Moltmann's claim that "what is stated by the name 'God' can be understandably demonstrated only when it is expressed in connection with a radical and, therefore, unavoidable, questionableness of reality."[7] When Lehmann uses Pauline images to describe the dynamics of reality as "bringing to naught the things that are, by the things that are not," he refers to a Christological claim for the transfiguring power of divine action. He describes God's action in Jesus Christ as "breaking in and breaking up the establishment."[8] As Lehmann sees it, to support the status quo is to deny the very structures of reality, for reality defined by the action of God in Jesus Christ always includes within it the constant pressure to change in the direction of freedom and humanization (*Transfiguration*, p. 5).

7. Christopher L. Morse, *The Logic of Promise in Moltmann's Theology* (Philadelphia: Fortress Press, 1979), p. 30. Moltmann justifies this claim under the rubric of promise. Christopher Morse has convincingly challenged and modified Moltmann's position employing a linguistic analysis of promise. While Lehmann does not use linguistic analysis to justify his claim, his understanding of divine action coupled with his use of apocalyptic themes would indeed benefit from such analysis. While Lehmann occasionally warns against the dangers of turning the analysis of language into a cult, he believes that a linguistic analysis of theological language would greatly benefit the theological endeavor, just as linguistic analysis of philosophical language has benefited philosophy. Lehmann himself, however, does not make such a move. His descriptions of revelation as a radical calling into question of present reality are just that — *descriptions* based on the Christian story as laid down in Scripture and handed down through the ages.

8. Lehmann, *The Transfiguration of Politics* (New York: Harper & Row, 1975), p. 80. All subsequent references to this volume will be made parenthetically in the text.

120

Although Lehmann equates divine action with this radical challenge to the status quo, he, like Paul, does not claim that every change that occurs in the world is a sign of divine revelation. He judges change to be a result of divine action whenever it produces humanization — that is, the freedom and limits necessary for human relatedness. Humanization is the fundamental act of God in relation to humanity, the act by which all transformations of human reality are judged. One can interpret change in the world as a product of divine revelation only when that change is consistent with God's humanizing activity in the cross and resurrection of Jesus Christ.

The term Lehmann uses to describe this apocalyptic interpretation of divine action is "transfiguration." Lehmann defines transfiguration in relation to two other types of change that form a sequence of escalating intensity. These types are used to describe a shift in the structures of human affairs. The first kind of change is transformation, which, according to Lehmann, indicates a shift from one type of power to another — for example, one avoids military action by employing negotiation. The second kind of change is transvaluation, which indicates that an accepted value has been inverted — for example, hatred, a valued emotion in relation to one's enemy, is inverted into love as the valued emotion toward an enemy (*Transfiguration*, p. 74). Transvaluation is more powerful than transformation, but transfiguration is a more thoroughgoing kind of change than either of these: it indicates a turning point in human events that creates entirely new structures for human relationships. In Lehmann's words, transfiguration indicates that one has broken out of "old, dehumanizing confinements into the direction of liberating possibilities" (*Transfiguration*, p. 76). Lehmann identifies "transfiguration" as the word that best describes the action of God. It indicates that divine action makes "room for freedom in so unfamiliar a sense as to take nothing less than a *metabasis eis allo genos* (a totally other foundation for things)" (*Transfiguration*, p. 78). Two examples of transfiguration will help uncover what Lehmann means by the term.

First, Lehmann uses the word "transfiguration" when existing power oversteps the "limits of tolerance" and a completely new power structure is brought into existence. Such was the case, he says, when Dietrich Bonhoeffer and his colleagues attempted to assassinate Hitler. "The patriot had to perform what in normal times is the action of a scoundrel. . . . 'Treason' had become true patriotism, and what was normally 'patriotism' had become treason."[9] In such a situation the order and value of actions are seen from a completely different perspective (*Transfiguration*, p. 75). Although the attempt on Hitler's life failed, it was an attempt in the direction of the transfiguration of politics.

Another example of transfiguration is found in J. Louis Martyn's description of the civil rights movement in the 1960s. On one side of the clash, Martyn reminds us, there were "Bull" Connor and men with whips and guns — the people who held all the power. On the other side of the clash stood Martin Luther King, Jr., and alongside him people with no whips or guns — in short, people with no power. In standing against the powers that supported the status quo, King and his followers effected a transfiguration of power. Those who fired the guns could not prevail against those who lived by God's grace.[10] Something was brought into existence that was not there before: justice, dignity, and a change in the structures of power.[11]

In both examples there is a radical change in the very foundation of power, a change that brings about humanization and is the result of the transfiguring act of God. In such situations human politics works on the side of divine politics to "make time and space make room for human freedom and fulfillment" (*Transfiguration*, p. 226).

9. Quoted by Lehmann in "Piety, Power, and Politics," *The Spire* 7, no. 2 (Summer 1982): 8.

10. Martyn, "From Paul to Flannery O'Connor," p. 14.

11. It is important to note that in the first example, the transfiguration of power involved participation in a violent act, while in the second example, transfiguration was the result of nonviolent civil disobedience. This leads one to ask whether Lehmann's apocalyptic perspective allows for Christian participation in violence. This issue will be addressed in Chapter Five, in which we will examine Lehmann's views on revolutionary activity.

Lehmann's identification of transfiguration with divine action has its foundation in the transfiguration passages of the Gospels of Matthew, Mark, and John. He specifically employs the poetic and political images from the transfiguration passage in the book of Matthew to describe revelation as standing in radical contradiction to present reality. This passage recounts the time when Jesus and three disciples retreated to a mountain during the Feast of Tabernacles. Moses and Elijah appeared and began to talk with Jesus. Then, we are told, "Jesus was transfigured." The Greek word for "transfiguration" is *metamorphousthai*. The word originally served the Hellenistic belief that deification of a person required that the soul and body be radically transformed from the human, mortal state to the immortal state of the gods. Such a metamorphosis into deity, however, has no place in the Christian message that "Jesus was transfigured." The meaning of *metamorphousthai*, says Lehmann, is not Hellenistic but apocalyptic. "It denotes the radical changes imminent in the world owing to a sudden foretaste of the long-promised and long-expected new world to come" (*Transfiguration*, p. 80).

Lehmann believes that the biblical account of the transfiguration of Jesus points to the "revolutionary character of reality" in that it is a "prodromal" sign of what is to come (*Transfiguration*, p. 80). From the Greek word *prodromos*, "prodromal" means "running along at headlong speed." According to Crane Brinton, prior to a revolution, "prodromal" signs act as indications to keen observers that a revolution is on its way. This, says Lehmann, is the type of sign we find in the story of the transfiguration of Jesus (*Transfiguration*, p. 313). It indicates that "time is running out" for the establishment and for all who support the status quo. In biblical, prophetic language, it indicates that "the time is at hand":

The question Whose world is this and by whose and what authority? is heading for the countdown and a liftoff in a blinding light of shattering presence and power after which the world never can and never will be the same again. A transfiguration — in this case, the Transfiguration — has happened! And neither history nor nature, society nor culture, nor man himself will be experienced as before, for they will not be as before. In the Transfiguration of Jesus of Nazareth, the Christ, the politics of God has transfigured the politics of man. (*Transfiguration*, p. 83)

Again, the meaning of divine politics intertwines with that of human politics. The "transfiguration of politics" indicates the bringing into being of that which did not exist before. There will be no "business as usual" when human politics has been transfigured by the politics of God. Human politics serves the politics of God when it yields to the pressure of "making room for God's freedom for man to be human in this world and the next" (*Transfiguration*, p. 85). The Transfiguration, in short, represents the end of the Old Age and the beginning of the New.

Some of Lehmann's critics charge that his reference to "God breaking in and breaking up the established order" is sloganeering devoid of concrete definition. When he uses this image, however, he refers to a theological concept with far more depth than mere slogan would allow. Divine revelation *is* the transfiguration of the world in accordance with the divine will. Although the world is created good, it has set out on a course contrary to providential intention. Apart from divine power, the world will remain as it is or change only in the same misguided direction, away from humanizing purpose. God's action, therefore, must be experienced as transfiguration. It will not, of course, be experienced as just *a* transfiguration but as that transfiguration which moves in the direction of God's movement described in the Old and New Testaments. The apocalyptic themes of divine lordship, the New Age, and the parousia further describe that transfiguration.

The Lordship of Christ

According to Ernst Käsemann, the fundamental apocalyptic question is "To whom does the sovereignty of the world belong?"[12] In the writings of Paul, the question of sovereignty uncovers a limited dualism in which the powers and principalities vie for lordship over creation.[13] Paul believes that human beings always have a lord — either the demonic powers or the Spirit of Jesus Christ. Käsemann describes Paul's understanding of lordship this way:

> Man for Paul is never just on his own. He . . . becomes . . . what he is by determination from outside, i.e., by the power which takes possession of him and the lordship to which he surrenders himself. His life is from the beginning a stake in the confrontation between God and the principalities of this world. In other words, it mirrors the cosmic contention for the lordship of the world and is its concretion. As such, man's life can only be understood apocalyptically.[14]

Human identity and action, therefore, are determined in answering the question "Who is the lord of our existence?" or "Whose slave are we?" For Paul the question of lordship is decisively answered in the apocalypse of Jesus Christ. There is no image of freedom in Paul's writings apart from the reality of lordship. Either we are in bondage to sin or we are freed by being slaves to Christ. For Paul, then, the question "Who is our lord?" becomes *the* ethical question. Paul's descriptions of sin and grace demonstrate the emphasis he places on lordship in defining human responsibility.

Paul does not see sin as simply a list of wrong acts. He often

12. Käsemann, "On the Subject of Primitive Christian Apocalyptic," pp. 135-36.

13. Martyn believes that an apt interpretation of Pauline apocalyptic is that of Flannery O'Connor: she claims that Paul is describing "the action of grace in territory held largely by the devil" (see "From Paul to Flannery O'Connor," p. 15).

14. Käsemann, "On the Subject of Primitive Christian Apocalyptic," p. 136. Käsemann's description of Paul anticipates a key assertion in Lehmann's ethic: responsible human action in a Christian context is parabolic behavior. Lehmann also believes, as Paul does, that "each life mirrors the cosmic contention for the lordship of the world"; hence each life becomes a living parable or image of divine action.

speaks of "sin" in the singular, describing it as a sphere of influence, a cosmic force, or a personified power. As Günther Bornkamm points out, sin is not simply something that we do; sin itself acts. Sin has "come into the world" (Rom. 5:12) and achieved dominion (Rom. 5:21). It is a power that enslaves (Rom. 7:14), and it exacts its wages in death (Rom. 6:23).[15]

Thus Paul can describe his own frustration at setting out to do the good and yet doing the very evil he seeks to avoid. He describes the self as enslaved to a power beyond its control, a self "sold under sin" (Rom. 7:14b). Clearly, Paul speaks of the self as performing the action here: "I do what I do not want" (Rom. 7:16). At the same time there is another actor on the scene, because sin directs the self's action: "It is no longer I that do it, but sin which dwells within me" (Rom. 7:17). "I, yet not I," Paul says, "commit sinful acts."

We also find this idea of "I, yet not I" in Paul's references to grace. He claims that he has worked hard, yet it is not he who has done the work, but Christ (1 Cor. 15:10). Our actions are directed by the one who is our lord: either the sin that dwells within us or the Christ who sets us free.

Accordingly, there is no such thing as a totally autonomous human decision. Human action can be understood not in and of itself but only in relation to the powers that vie for lordship over human existence. There are no human actions apart from the powers that rule us. This does not mean that we are reduced to marionettes with no will of our own. But it does mean that the self always acts in relation to a power beyond itself. Furthermore, to reiterate Käsemann's point, Paul believes that each life "mirrors the cosmic contention for the lordship of the world." We become, he says, its "concretion" — the embodiment of that struggle.[16]

Lehmann's work follows that of the apostle Paul in claiming

15. Bornkamm, *Paul* (New York: Harper & Row, 1971), p. 133.
16. This notion coincides with Lehmann's understanding of responsible Christian action as "parabolic" action, a concept subsequently discussed in this chapter.

that the primary moral question is "Who is our Lord?" In responding to this question, we learn who we are, who God is, and how we are to live together in humanizing community.

From the outset, however, a serious challenge to the concept of divine lordship must be addressed. Lehmann knows that the concept of lordship has been called into question by proponents of feminist theology. Some feminist theologians object that the image of Christ as Lord, similar to the image of God as Father, perpetuates a long and exclusive list of masculine images for God. When this is the only objection, simply switching to the neutral term "sovereign" takes care of the problem.

Other theologians, however, do not simply object to "Lord" as a masculine designation for God. They find in the very idea of sovereignty an oppressive image of domination that grows out of any hierarchically structured relationship. These theologians believe that the domination of oppressor over oppressed — rich over poor, white over black, men over women — that exists in society is both reflected in the Godhead and confirmed by it when we refer to God as "Lord."[17]

While recognizing that the doctrine of the sovereignty of God has been misused to serve oppressive purposes, Lehmann asserts that the image, properly interpreted, is a liberating one. In agreement with Karl Barth, Lehmann claims that recognition of God as the only Lord indicates that no human being can legitimately become lord over another. Thus we are given the foundation on which to fight against those who seek to oppress others in society. Furthermore, to confess that God is all-powerful is to affirm Christ's victory over the powers and principalities that seek to enslave us. Rather than indicating an isolated, independent, and aloof God, the sovereignty and self-sufficiency of God indicate that God chose to create humanity out of love rather than necessity. Like Barth, Lehmann believes that "God chose not to be alone." God "created

17. The logic of the arguments is that since God is masculine, the image of God's will on earth becomes one in which the masculine lord dominates the feminine subject.

a world fit to be human in" out of free and unconditional love.[18]

For Lehmann, the doctrine of lordship leads once again to humanization, whereby human maturity and reciprocated love require "not the abandonment of transcendence [lordship], but a fresh, meaningful, and integrating connection between transcendence and humanity."[19] The challenge issued by feminist theology is properly met not by discarding the idea of lordship but by rightly interpreting it, so that divine lordship itself indicates forgiveness, justice, and reconciliation among human beings. Lehmann's interpretation of lordship informs his understanding of the place held by the doctrine of providence in Christian ethics, the function of the human conscience, and the definition of ethics as something other than a search for the highest good.

Providence. According to Lehmann, the doctrine of providence affects our understanding of two aspects of reality: power and limits. On the one hand, it informs our understanding of power by describing God's action as that which sustains the world by changing it. Human association can be sustained only through constant transformation in the direction of Christ's cross and resurrection. On the other hand, the doctrine of providence informs our understanding of limits by demonstrating that certain parameters are necessary in order for human beings to live in association with one another. The doctrine of providence, therefore, defines the essential aspect of reality as "persistence of [divine] intention" that places limits on human existence.[20] The

18. Lehmann, "The Decalogue and the Parameters of a Human Future," paper delivered at the 1981 ACPE Conference entitled "Making and Keeping Human Life Human" (New York: ACPE Interchurch Center, 1981), p. 2. See also "The Commandments and the Common Life," *Interpretation*, Oct. 1980, pp. 341-55.

19. Lehmann, "A Christian Alternative to Natural Law," in *Die moderne Demokratie und ihr Recht: Festschrift für Gerhard Leibholz,* first ed., ed. Karl Dietrich Bracher et al. (Tübingen: J. C. B. Mohr [Paul Siebeck], 1966), p. 527.

20. Lehmann, "Religion, Power, and Christian Faith," in *Religion and Culture: Essays in Honor of Paul Tillich,* ed. Walter Leibrecht (New York:

following discussion examines Lehmann's understanding of providence in relation to power and limits.

Providence and Power. Lehmann sets out to demonstrate the religious character of power by first comparing the vision of the primitive world, which viewed power as essentially religious, with the vision of the contemporary world, which views power as essentially natural. The primitive world, Lehmann says, believed that the gods controlled the operation of nature. Since no single unifying sense of purpose could be located in nature, a "limited polytheism" (such as the pantheon) served the primitive mind. Power was, therefore, understood as a religious phenomenon. The contemporary world, on the other hand, seeks to understand and control power through science and technology by organizing power into predictable patterns and laws. One no longer looks *beyond* the operation of power but *into* the operation of power to understand it ("Religion," pp. 243, 245). Thus power is understood not as a religious phenomenon but as a natural phenomenon. It provokes not a sense of dependence but a sense of adventure.

In Lehmann's assessment, contemporary society correctly sees that power is "a question of energy, not divinities." It rightly believes that we must seek to understand and control power through scientific exploration. The *primitive* mind, however, was correct in believing that transcendence is required to give meaningful purpose to human life. The contemporary mind errs at precisely this point, for it fails to recognize that effective control of power also involves questions of authority and purpose, questions regarding who has the authority over power and for what purpose it is being employed. The contemporary world fails to understand that the problem of power is not just a problem of technology and control but also a problem of human existence, purpose, and destiny ("Religion," pp. 244, 247).

According to Lehmann, this oversight was brought into focus by the bombing of Hiroshima in August 1945.[21] Neither

---

Harper & Brothers, 1954), p. 246. All subsequent references to this essay will be made parenthetically in the text.

21. Lehmann says, "It was as though the bomb that fell on Hiroshima

the gods of primitive polytheism nor the science of contemporary culture could control such an unyielding force of power. The devastation wreaked by the bombing demonstrated that the contemporary attempt to control the threat of the forces of nature had failed. The attack unleashed a power that not only did not make room for being human but also threatened the very existence of humanity. The bombing of Hiroshima provided clear evidence that the control of power needs an understanding of divine lordship in order for power to serve human existence.

The most acute problem of power arises when power *fails* to serve the purposes of human existence. "Power that cannot be bounded by purpose," Lehmann points out, "threatens existence with meaninglessness and annihilation; purposes that fail of integration with the organized energies of existence lose persuasiveness and point" ("Religion," p. 248). One of the tasks of religion, Lehmann says, is to find the connection between power and the purposes of human existence.

Religion itself, however, sometimes abuses power. On the one hand, religion can identify itself too closely with power in order to further its own causes. As examples Lehmann cites Catholicism's sacerdotal interpretation of the world and Calvinistic theocracy ("Religion," p. 250).[22] On the other hand, it can allow power itself to become religion, thereby justifying the pursuit of power for power's sake. As examples of this problem Lehmann cites totalitarianism and some of the abuses of democracy.

A *constructive* relationship between power and religion occurs

---

had torn the scales from its eyes and a long-forgotten dimension of reality had been suddenly apprehended as too clearly inescapable and too dimly understood. Fear and anxiety lent critical urgency to the questions of the meaning and the purpose of existence. One felt an unspoken and impatient longing for some sign of deliverance to be supplied by religion. This could be the one alternative to futility" ("Religion, Power, and the Christian Faith," p. 246).

22. Through sacerdotalism the church claims a monopoly on sacred energy that resides in the sacraments, the priesthood, and papal infallibility. Through this monopoly on power, it seeks to bend public life to the authority of the church. In Calvinistic theocracy, the magistrates sought to force conformity on public life by imposing the Ten Commandments on society.

whenever religion gives "motivation and meaning to the energy and the authority" by which everything happens in the world: "It is this enabling and enlightening function of religion," Lehmann says, "which integrates the organized energies with the insistent purposes of existence, the relentless momentum of change with the equally relentless persistence of pattern and direction, or order and meaning, in, with, and under change." Religion accomplishes these tasks by enabling us to endure the world, but it does so by giving us the power to change the world ("Religion," p. 254). The problem of power is resolved when the energies and authority of power are given meaningful purpose.

Lehmann believes that the Christian affirmation of divine lordship recognizes that God alone supplies meaningful purpose to power. Change, in the form of transfiguration, indicates that God's sovereign control is pressuring events in the direction of meaningful purpose — that is, in the direction of humanization. This directional pressure does not reside in the inherent nature of things, as sacerdotalism claims. Nor does it arise from the imposition of law, as theocracy says. Power, as the prophets understood, is righteous will. "Upon this will the world depends for its existence and fulfillment," Lehmann points out. "And when the energies and the sovereignties of life are organized and expressed in accordance with this righteous will, they give to life both security and meaning" ("Religion," p. 254).

The Christian faith, therefore, understands the lordship of Christ to provide meaningful purpose to power. Jesus is the fulfillment of the prophetic tradition's understanding of power:

> He is, indeed, its fulfillment because he takes up, in and over the world, the actual exercise of power according to the will and purpose of God Himself. In the New Testament, as well as in the thought of the Church, Jesus is viewed not only as the unique revelation of God and the saviour of men and the world. He is also acknowledged as the lord of life. It is this integration of deity, deliverance, and lordship in the person and work of Jesus Christ that gives to Christian faith its constructive relation to the problem of power. ("Religion," pp. 254-55)

131

God in Jesus Christ reveals that our lives are not under the control of fate but are given meaning and purpose by divine will. To live within that purpose, Lehmann says, is to live by grace.

Providence and Limits. Providence not only changes the world but also defines the limits that make human life possible. One way in which providence sets limits is through the Law. The Law, however, sets limits by serving a *descriptive* rather than a *prescriptive* function. According to Lehmann, the Decalogue, for instance, is a product of divine providence that set limits or parameters around human life — in other words, the laws mark off the area in which humanization can occur. Obedience to the Decalogue does not mean following "a calculus of permissions and prohibitions." The Decalogue is descriptive in that it indicates divine pressure upon reality toward purposeful limits in the form of both change and order. For Lehmann this means that the Decalogue is "at once parabolic and paradigmatic of what God is doing in the world to make room for the freedom and fulfillment which being human takes."[23]

Lehmann makes this distinction between description and prescription by using two of Karl Barth's terms, "Law as Gospel" and "Gospel as Law." Although the designations themselves can be confusing, the distinction Lehmann is making is important.

"Gospel as Law" designates the positive interpretation of the relationship between Gospel and Law. For the Gospel to take the form of Law — such as the Ten Commandments, the Sermon on the Mount, and the parenetic sections of the Pauline epistles — means simply that the Gospel sets parameters around human life. We live within the parameters marked off by, or described by, the Gospel as Law. One interprets the Law in a flexible fashion, attempting to understand the spirit rather than the letter of it. In fact, the letter of the Law — the legalistic, prescriptive interpretation of the Law — moves us out of the realm of the Gospel altogether.[24]

---

23. Lehmann, "The Decalogue and the Parameters of a Human Future," p. 16.
24. Ibid., pp. 2-3.

"Law as Gospel" designates the negative interpretation of the relationship between Gospel and Law. It indicates that the Law assumes a primary place in Christian proclamation. Interpretation of divine activity is reduced to law-giving. Even though those who follow this position also seek to follow the spirit of the Law, they fall short by employing a prescriptive interpretation of Law. With this interpretation the Law tends to be less flexible. Rather than marking off the space in which we live, it imposes a more rigid order. In this view, Lehmann believes, the Commandments disintegrate into prescription, memorization, and a "calculus of permissions and prohibitions."[25]

Lehmann believes that the Christian Gospel demands that priority be given to the action of God as Lord rather than to commandments and rules. Divine commandments are signs of God's providential ordering of the world. Refusing to interpret the Bible as a set of prescriptions, Lehmann interprets the Commandments in a way that is consistent with his hermeneutic, which views the Bible as offering parabolic images. The Commandments, he says, "are not prescriptions, but parables." Furthermore, they are parables which indicate that humanity does not live under the blind hand of fate but has a purpose.[26] Several examples will demonstrate Lehmann's emphasis on lordship and the *descriptive* nature of the Commandments.

Lehmann's reflection on the First Commandment, "Thou shalt have no other gods before me," concentrates not on the *prescription* regarding monotheism but on a *description* of "what

25. Ibid.
26. The parameters established when the Gospel takes the form of the Law have to do with both the relationship between human beings and God and human beings' relationships with one another: "The right hand tablet (first three Commandments) directs us in the parameters of responsibility towards God. The left hand tablet directs us in the parameters of reciprocal responsibility toward our neighbor. The right tablet tells us what is involved in a realistic, liberating, and fulfilling commitment between God and human beings. The left tablet tells us what is involved in a realistic, liberating, and fulfilling commitment between persons and among persons as neighbors" ("The Decalogue and the Parameters of a Human Future," pp. 15-16).

it means to have a God." Lehmann believes that in pointing to God, alongside of whom there is no other, the First Commandment describes God as the authority who can be trusted. "God is the authority upon whom humanity utterly depends and in whom humanity utterly trusts," he declares.[27] Because God has created the world "fit to be human in," divine authority indicates that we have been entrusted to God's care, which creates humanizing relationships.

Another example of the descriptive task of the Commandments, Lehmann says, is found in the commandment against taking the Lord's name in vain. This commandment does not *proscribe* swearing but *describes* life in relation to transcendence. Like Luther, Lehmann interprets the commandment to mean that we must "not go about as if God's name were useless." It is not in everyday swearing that we break the commandment but in living as if we do not know the name of God, or as if the name of God made no difference in human life.

In a similar way, the commandment to "Keep the Sabbath holy" is not a *prohibition* against working on Sundays but an *indication* that this God whose authority produces humanization has given us creation as a gift that elicits gratitude and demands recognition of boundaries. According to Lehmann, gratitude provides a check against indifference to the world, and recognition of divinely ordained limits provides a check against exploitation.

This gratitude for God's creative activity encompasses human gratitude for one another. In describing "what it means to have a God," all of the Commandments describe human relationships built on reciprocal responsibility, whereby each human being is responsible not only for the self but also for others and for the whole of creation. Being placed in humanizing relationship means that we are accountable to one another for a responsibility that holds human relationships in trust. The Commandments describe what is necessary for humanization to occur.

27. Ibid., pp. 18-19.

To summarize, divine providence provides us with the power to endure the world by changing it in the direction of God's will. Providence also provides us with limits through the Commandments, which describe genuinely *human* life. At the heart of this description lies the image of human relationships that depend on reciprocal responsibility. Lehmann has further developed this idea of providence, limits, and reciprocal responsibility in his interpretation of the human conscience.[28]

28. The idea of reciprocal responsibility is also explored in his soon-to-be-published manuscript entitled "The Decalogue and a Human Future." Relying in part on the sociological analyses of Peter Blau and Louis Dumont to reflect on the structures of human relationship that best serve humanization, Lehmann clearly rejects both hierarchy and egalitarianism. Hierarchical distribution of power, which ranks people according to privilege, results in inequality and injustice. Egalitarianism, on the other hand, which has been proposed as the foil to hierarchy, tends to define equality as uniformity — that is, it states that in order for persons to be *equal,* they must be perceived as being *alike.* Egalitarianism, therefore, fails to take adequate account of the differences among people. In egalitarianism "what counts is all the ways in which others are like ourselves, not the claims of others upon ourselves to take responsibility for difference" (p. 63).

Autonomy and individual rights become the principles necessary for upholding the egalitarian ideal:

> The egalitarian ideal . . . is rooted in an individualism which regards difference as exigenous rather than as indigenous to the human condition. Hence the *modus vivendi* according to which everybody is accorded the right to pursue his or her own rights, so long as such pursuit does not interfere with the rights of others. (p. 64).

Lehmann concludes that "neither hierarchical nor egalitarian social, economic, cultural and political structures are capable of furthering the freedom which being human in this world takes" (p. 42). Lehmann proposes that the *tertium quid* between hierarchy and egalitarianism is heterogeneity. Here hierarchy is recognized as inequality; the equality of the egalitarian ideal is replaced with heterogeneity — that is, a recognition of the differences that exist among human beings. Furthermore, the relationship between inequality and heterogeneity is identified as reciprocal responsibility (p. 72).

By way of illustrating Lehmann's position, one can point to women's struggle for equality in our society. Whenever that struggle takes the form of an egalitarian protest against hierarchy, one bases the argument for equality on the notion that men and women are the same in every respect except bodily function. On the other hand, whenever the protest against the in-

The Human Conscience. Lehmann's understanding of lord-ship, the relationship of providence to power and limits, and the relationship of reciprocal responsibility that providence creates leads him to redescribe the role played by the human conscience in ethical decisions. The individual's conscience operates properly only when set in relationship to divine lord-ship and to the conscience of the neighbor.

Lehmann says the etymology of the word "conscience" points to a concept of relationship. The Latin *con-scientia* includes a root that means "knowing" and a prefix that means "relation." Conscience, therefore, indicates some kind of "knowing-in-relation." The question, of course, becomes "Knowing what, in relation to whom?"[29] Lehmann says philosophical and theological ethics have made two primary errors in answering the question raised by the etymological study. The first error involves defining the conscience in the context of the self's relation to itself — that is, the conscience is an individual, internalized function which gives each person the ability to choose between good and evil on his or her own. This, Lehmann says, is an *autonomous* definition of the conscience. The second error involves interpreting the conscience *heteronomously*. According to this interpretation, the conscience links the agent to a system of order imposed from outside. One knows what is right or wrong in relation to a system of rules. Against these two interpretations Lehmann proposes a *theonomous* relationship to define the conscience. In other words, the conscience recognizes good and evil in relation to God's humaniz-ing activity, which puts the individual in relationship with the neighbor (*Ethics*, pp. 348-49).

---

equalities of hierarchy is based on an affirmation of heterogeneity, one celebrates the differences between men and women while affirming the responsibility they have for one another. This move away from hierarchy and egalitarianism, Lehmann claims, is consistent with the description of human relations found in the Ten Commandments. (See also "Command-ments and the Common Life," *Interpretation*, October 1980, pp. 341-55).

29. Lehmann, *Ethics in a Christian Context* (New York: Harper & Row, 1963), p. 348. All subsequent references to this volume will be made parenthetically in the text.

Lehmann traces the history of the place given to the conscience in ethics, identifying four major stages: the conscience as "the enemy of humanization," as found in Greek tragedy; "the domestication of conscience," as found in Aquinas; the conscience as "duty's inner citadel," so defined by Kant; and "the dethronement of conscience" by Sigmund Freud. Before we turn to Lehmann's own proposal, a brief summary of his account of this history is in order.

First, Lehmann explains that the conscience is "the enemy of humanization" in Greek tragedy, because in it the conscience has a completely negative function. By inducing guilt, the conscience judges an action negatively after the action has taken place. Second, Lehmann explains that Aquinas retained this negative function of the conscience but added a positive function as well. According to Aquinas, the conscience serves casuistry by aiding the agent in applying universal principles to particular situations. In this way the conscience has the positive function of instructing the agent in what to do. It still, however, retains the function of judging an action to be right or wrong upon reflection after the fact. Given its positive function, the conscience has become bearable; hence Lehmann's designation of Aquinas' definition of the conscience as "the domestication of conscience."

Third, Lehmann points out that Kant assigned these same two functions to the conscience — that of applying universal principles to particular cases and that of judging an action after the fact. However, whereas Aquinas defined the conscience as an internal voice of human reason, Kant believed it to be an internal voice of a transcendental ideal. Nevertheless, according to Lehmann, Kant unintentionally prepared the way for the decline of the conscience. In seeking to define the conscience as the link between humanity's internal nature and the external order that sustains human life, Kant presented the conscience as "an internal voice of an external authority." However, it is this "authoritarian conscience," says Lehmann, "which has so conspicuously lost its ethical persuasiveness and force today" (*Ethics*, p. 336).

Finally, according to Lehmann, Freud brought about "the dethronement of conscience" through his inability to find such a positive function within the human being. According to Freud, one's inner voice, whether it originates from oneself or from God, does not lead one to make moral decisions. It leads only to an overwhelming and crippling sense of guilt. Responding to Kant's alleged statement that evidence of God's greatness is found in "the starry heavens above" and "the moral law within," Freud claimed that "the stars are unquestionably superb, but where conscience is concerned God has been guilty of an uneven and careless piece of work" (cited in *Ethics*, p. 337).

Lehmann, who understands the conscience from the perspective of the lordship of Christ, says it has to do with "relational" knowledge. Understood relationally, the conscience is not an internal characteristic of human nature that condemns specific actions. "It is not the conscience," Lehmann says, "but the Lord who judges" (*Ethics*, pp. 353, 355). The conscience refers to one's knowledge of the boundaries set by God for human existence, a knowledge that can be grasped only in relation to the neighbor.

By way of illustration, Lehmann points to the passage in Corinthians regarding the question of whether one can eat meat that has been offered to idols. Paul believes that the law prohibiting such action carries no weight for Christians. Because idols are "no-beings" who have no existence, eating meat sacrificed to them carries no idolatrous implications. Nevertheless, one must not eat such meat if doing so causes a weaker neighbor to stumble. Paul, therefore, describes the conscience as free from prescriptive rules but bound by concern for the neighbor. This, Lehmann says, is what he means by a "theonomous conscience":

> The theonomous conscience is the conscience immediately sensitive to the freedom of God to do in the always changing human situation what his humanizing aims and purposes require. The theonomous conscience is governed and directed by the freedom of God alone. . . . The concrete instance of the theonomous conscience is the pre-eminent claim of my neighbor's conscience upon and over my own. (*Ethics*, pp. 358-59)

This does not mean that the neighbor's conscience can function as a new kind of law. It does, however, indicate that the conscience describes a relation whereby human beings have claims upon one another. The basis of those claims is God's political, humanizing activity revealed in the lordship of Jesus Christ.

An Alternative to Defining Ethics as the Search for the Good. As Lehmann sees it, the tendency of Christian theologians to shift their attention from an examination of divine activity and its impact on Christian action toward an examination of the *summum bonum* represents a diversion from their true task (*Ethics*, p. 166). Indeed, Lehmann devotes a large section of *Ethics in a Christian Context* to analyzing the tradition of Christian ethics in the West that defines ethics as the search for the *summum bonum*. To claim that ethics ought not to involve a search for the good represents a radical shift away from the way Christian ethics is generally understood. This shift is best seen in Lehmann's evaluation of Aristotle, whose philosophical ethics has had a great impact on Christian ethics.

Aristotle defines the highest good as happiness, and happiness as "an activity of the soul in accordance with perfect virtue." Consequently, he gives most of his attention to an analysis of the nature of virtue According to Aristotle, virtue, particularly the virtue of prudence, teaches us to choose wisely between extremes. Thus from Aristotle we receive the rule of the "golden mean." In Lehmann's opinion, "the achievement of goodness is, for Aristotle, no counsel of perfection, but a pragmatically calculated more and less, compounded of reasoning and perception" (*Ethics*, pp. 168, 170).

We find in Aristotle and the tradition he has bequeathed to Christian ethics what so many critics claim is missing in Lehmann's ethics — "pragmatically calculated reasoning." Some critics argue that virtue, particularly the virtue of prudence, is what Lehmann's ethic lacks, and without it his ethic has a random character which leaves the agent without any concrete idea of what to do in any given situation.

Lehmann believes, however, that the fundamental problem with defining ethics as a search for the good with an emphasis

139

on the virtue of prudence is that it leads to "the complete domestication of evil" (*Ethics*, p. 170).[30] In other words, prudence or common sense as an ethical category cannot adequately challenge the power of evil. Furthermore, it is not always the prudent decision that squares with the Christian faith. We are not always called upon to do that which makes the most sense. Sometimes we are called upon to do what appears foolish to others. The idea of following a crucified God, for instance, does not fall in line with the dictates of common sense; it is not a "prudent" act. This is not to say that Christianity is irrational or that we are called upon to be utter fools. Nevertheless, we follow the dictates of the cross, not of common sense.

According to Lehmann, the result of Christ's victory on the cross is not that we now have the freedom to choose between good and evil. Ethics is centered not in knowing what is the good but in knowing who is our Lord. It is not a matter of choice but a matter of apocalyptic perspective — knowing who is the Lord of our existence and whose side we are on. By destroying the powers that enslave us, Christ gives us the power to live as new creatures freed from the tyranny of illegitimate lords and free to live in humanizing relationships with one another. In other words, Christ calls us to live at the turn of the ages, another characteristic feature of Pauline apocalyptic that coincides with Lehmann's ethics.

Living at the Turn of the Ages

While Paul fights the enthusiasts who believe that the New Age has fully arrived, he nevertheless believes that the turning of the ages has already begun. He stands among those "upon whom

30. According to Lehmann, "It is intrinsic to the preoccupation of the Nicomachean ethics with the search for the good that evil is a parenthetical concern. It is recognized and alluded to but not wrestled with and worried about. Evil is at best an epiphenomenal delay which does not, indeed cannot, seriously impede the Nicomachean program for training in virtue" (*Ethics*, p. 171).

the end of the ages has come" (1 Cor. 10:11) and among those who know that "the form of this world is passing away" (1 Cor. 7:31). According to Paul, a "new space" — to use J. Louis Martyn's term — has been created within the world by the death and resurrection of Jesus Christ. Martyn explains that according to Paul, certain distinctions that had always existed in the world have, with the life, death and resurrection, and expected return of Christ, been destroyed: "There was a world whose fundamental structures were certain pairs of opposites: circumcision/uncircumcision; Jew/Gentile; slave/free; male/female. . . . Those who have been baptized into Christ, however, know that, in Christ, that world does not any longer have real existence."[31] In contrast to the distinctions of the Old Age, unity marks the New World created by Christ: "You are all one in Christ Jesus" (Gal. 3:28). With Christ's life, death, and resurrection a new reality enters the world and all reality is fundamentally changed. Thus one begins to understand what is meant by the claim that God's revelation is the transfiguration of the world. The turn of the ages indicates, as Lehmann says, that the "transfiguration" of the world is underway.[32]

Signs of the New Age, however, are now hidden in the Old Age and thus require new vision in order to be seen. We are not naturally equipped with the vision necessary to see and therefore choose the way of life in the world. Martyn points out that Paul, standing at the turn of the ages, speaks of a new way of knowing that is not ours by nature but ours as a gift of the Spirit. According to Martyn, however, Paul does not speak of knowing

31. Martyn, "Apocalyptic Antinomies in Paul's Letter to the Galatians," *New Testament Studies* 31 (1 July 1985): 415.

32. Transfiguration, according to Lehmann, means "the ingression of 'things that are not' into the 'things that are,' so that man may come abreast of God's next move in giving human shape to human life." Lehmann says that the turn of the ages does not only mean that the world will be experienced or perceived differently. More importantly, it means that history, nature, society, culture, and humanity "will not be as before." There is an ontological shift in the structures that make up the world. Jesus Christ's presence in the human story means that things will never be the same again (*Transfiguration*, p. 76).

according to the New Age but of knowing according to the cross.[33]

Using the image of the two lenses of bifocals, one to sharpen "near vision" and the other to sharpen "far vision," Martyn suggests that apocalyptic vision enables us to see "near things and far things." Such "bifocal vision" helps us understand what it means to have inherited both "the suffering world" and "the triumphant Hallelujah Chorus."[34] There are people in the world who actually cannot see suffering around them. But by knowing according to the cross, we can look at the world and see the suffering: "Who is weak, and I am not weak? Who is made to fall, and I am not indignant?" (2 Cor. 11:29). Our "near vision" enables us to see that a war is raging between God and the powers of death. There are other people in the world, however, who cannot see anything *but* suffering. But by knowing according to the cross, we can look at the world and see hope: "The sufferings of this present time are not worth comparing with the glory that is to be revealed to us" (Rom. 8:18). Our "far vision" enables us to see the outcome of the battle, to see the resurrection. By knowing the world according to the cross, we see both suffering and hope.

Through apocalyptic vision we are enabled to see both the war and the outcome of the battle. Paul is not, however, proposing an "interim ethic" showing us how to live in the Old Age before the New Age arrives. Although we must be alert to the dangers of enthusiasm, we nevertheless live *now* in that "new space" created by the powerful invasion of Christ. Living within that new space, we can no longer tolerate Old Age distinctions in the social and political order that oppress and destroy. We refuse to allow the political order that has foundations in the Old Age to operate under the slogan "business as usual" because we do not recognize its legitimacy in God's world. It is in that

33. Martyn, "Epistemology at the Turn of the Ages: 2 Corinthians 5.16," in *Christian History and Interpretation: Studies Presented to John Knox*, ed. W. R. Farmer et al. (Cambridge: Cambridge University Press, 1967), pp. 269-87.

34. Ibid., pp. 12, 10.

new space created in Christ that the church is called into being and action.

The language of "new creation" or "new age" is essential to Pauline apocalyptic. A critical question for Paul and his listeners revolved around the extent to which they believed that the New Age had arrived. "Enthusiasts" during Paul's time believed that because the age had so fully arrived, they no longer were held accountable for the state of the world. Some have interpreted Paul's position by saying that he offers us an "interim ethic," that he teaches us to live between the times.

Lehmann holds to an idea similar to that of an "interim ethic" when discussing Paul's view of the New Age in Romans 13. Lehmann says we can understand what it means to be "obliged to submit" to governing authorities only from the perspective of Jesus' inauguration of the New Age in the midst of the Old. With Anders Nygren, Lehmann argues that in Romans 13 Paul warns against the spiritualists' attempt to live fully within the New Age. To embrace life in the New Age fully means to fall into the errors of anarchy. Because this world cannot fully sustain the New Age, living by the order of the Old Age is to some extent still necessary (*Transfiguration*, p. 37).

Here Lehmann has taken an unfortunate turn. Anarchy is not the sign of the New Age, nor does the New Age require the sustenance of Old Age distinctions to keep it alive in the "real" world. Lehmann's own image of the authority of God that both binds and frees, offering liberating limits for human existence, is characteristic of the New Age itself. As Paul saw it, the New Age never meant anarchy but provided the limits necessary to make freedom possible.

J. Louis Martyn poses a solution to the dilemma of enthusiasm with his notion of a "new space." Disclaiming the idea of an "interim ethic," Martyn says the New Age invades the Old and creates within it this "new space." It is there in that new space created by the gospel that the church dwells and lives by the standards of the New Age. Hence, while we still live within the context of the Old Age, we live by the standards of the New.

This interpretation is much more consistent with Lehmann's

ethic than the idea of an "interim ethic."[35] Lehmann himself employs the image of space when he defines both ethics and the classical study of politics as describing that "space" in which humanity can live together in harmony. Lehmann also points to others who have used the image of space to describe human freedom. Thomas Jefferson hoped for "a body politic which guarantees *space* where freedom can appear."[36] Thus in its emphasis on the provision of "space" for the living of human life, Lehmann's theological ethic is consistent with Pauline apocalyptic claims for the New Age. In that new space created by Christ, the *koinonia* is called into being and action. Theology reflects upon and describes the conditions within that space.[37]

Perhaps more than any other image, the image of space

35. It is also more consistent with his interpretation of the transfiguration of Jesus as a "prodromal" event. The image of the transfigured Jesus anticipates the transfiguration of human politics and human relations that takes place as the New Age is inaugurated by Christ.

36. The Duc de la Rochefoucauld-Liancourt told Louis XVI that the public realm, which had always been reserved for those who were free from the fundamental cares and needs of life, "*should offer its space* and its light to the immense majority who are not free." And recently Hannah Arendt referred to "the *space* of men's free deeds and living words which could endow life with splendor" (my italics; see Lehmann, *Transfiguration,* pp. 4, 9, 8).

37. Lehmann's description of the *koinonia* within that "space" created by God's humanizing, political action coincides with J. Christiaan Beker's interpretation of Paul's apocalyptic view of the church. In the midst of a society that lives according to Old Age distinctions, Bekker says, Paul describes the church as providing "pockets" of a new life (Bekker, *Paul the Apostle: The Triumph of God in Life and Thought* [Philadelphia: Fortress Press, 1980], p. 326). The members of the church are to be "blameless and innocent, children of God without blemish in the midst of a crooked and perverse generation, among whom [they] shine as lights in the world" (Phil. 2:15). The church fights the powers and principalities by refusing to live according to their ways. Paul's view on mutuality in marriage and his eradication of racial, social, and sexual distinctions in the church run counter to those of his society. (See 1 Cor. 7:3-5 and Gal. 3:28.) The church is to live in a different way, in a different and yet overlapping sphere and age. "Old Age" distinctions are not allowed as the church fulfills its apocalyptic vocation in the world. At the same time, the church recognizes that Old Age distinctions continue to exist in the world and in the church as signs of sin.

144

summarizes Lehmann's method for theological ethics. Every aspect of his method represents an attempt to describe life within that space created by God's political, humanizing activity. Hence Lehmann says the task of ethics is "descriptive." That "space" which ethics describes provides the context for responsible human action. Hence Lehmann says that ethics is "contextual." The apocalyptic story of God's action on behalf of creation describes the pressure of divine purpose upon the existing reality to yield to the freedom and order necessary to sustain human life within that "space." Hence Lehmann says that ethics has both a narrative and an apocalyptic character.

Given its importance, the image of "space" cannot be dismissed as "only" a metaphorical image in Lehmann's ethics. Describing life within the new space created by God's invasion into the world of "time and space and things" lies at the heart of his ethics. Furthermore, life within that space reflects not only God's past and continuous actions on our behalf but also God's promised destiny for all of human life.

The Expectation of an Imminent Parousia

It is this fourth characteristic of Pauline apocalyptic — the expectation of an imminent parousia — that we would most expect to hear about in a discussion regarding apocalyptic. However ambiguous the term "apocalyptic" is, the expectation of the end of the world has long been associated with it and even classified as its key characteristic.

While the expectation of the imminent end of the world may be apocalyptic, it is not without qualification Christian apocalyptic. Apocalyptic expectation is used in the secular and the pseudo-Christian realm to refer exclusively to the destruction of the world. Thus the popular film *Apocalypse Now* portrays the end of the civilized world in the context of the atrocities of war. In like manner, apocalyptic passages in the Bible are often equated with the threat of nuclear destruction. The use of the word "apocalypse" or "apocalyptic" in these instances carries the message that the end of the world is imminent and that the revelation regarding the end is clearly given to all who have eyes to see. These instances, however, cannot be equated with Christian apocalyptic because they are divorced from the proclamation of Christ's death, resurrection, and Second Coming.

While Paul clearly expects an imminent parousia, at no point in his thought can we find the expectation of the end divorced from the destiny of Jesus Christ (see 1 Thess. 4:15–5:10; 1 Cor. 15:24). Unlike those whose apocalyptic expectations focus on destruction, Paul regards the end of the ages not with despair but with hope. For that reason, we can never equate the apocalyptic passages in the Bible with the threat of nuclear war or with any human destruction of creation. As Paul makes clear, the imminent parousia is not brought on by human foolishness or error but is determined solely by God.

Having distinguished Paul's expectation of an imminent parousia from secular and pseudo-Christian ones, we still face a problem in appropriating Paul's thought for today. The ongoing experience of time and history probably serves as a stronger hindrance to the appropriation of apocalyptic thought than any other. How do we deal with the fact that the end of the ages did not occur according to expectations? How can we possibly take seriously Paul's admonition to "stay awake" and to be alert with anticipation when 1900 years have passed since Paul spoke them?

The most popular solution to this dilemma proposes that we reinterpret Paul's mythological understanding of the parousia by moving its reference from the cosmic to the internal, existential realm. While the kingdom of God did not occur in history, it can be encountered in each successive moment by the individual who is exhorted to remain always open to the promises of God. In similar fashion we can admit that while Paul was wrong about the rapidity with which the parousia was approaching, we encounter the truth behind his expectation when we contemplate our own impending death. We can claim that the threat of individual death serves the same purpose as Paul's expectation of the imminent Day of the Lord. Our death calls each of us to be decisive and repentant in the present while God promises us future glory in our own resurrection in the next world.

Lehmann, however, does not rely on these two interpretations in order to find significance in Paul's expectation of an imminent parousia. Such interpretations undercut the *cosmic* force of the gospel Paul preaches, and so lead ethics down an individualistic path that Lehmann will not follow. Paul was indeed mistaken about the nearness of the end, but he said himself that we cannot know the time or the season (1 Thess. 5:1-2). Lehmann's theological ethic demonstrates that the ethical significance of the Second Coming of Christ is not destroyed by its delay. We can in fact identify two major consequences of the expectation of the Second Coming for theological ethics that Lehmann has appropriated.

First, the significance of Paul's image of the Second Coming lies in our inheritance of an ethic of hope. Hope, not guilt or fear, defines who we are and what we are to do. The promise held out by the Second Coming of Christ is, to quote Rubem Alves, that the "overwhelming brutality of facts that oppress" us in this present age does not have the last word, has not said all there is to say.[38] Hope reminds us that although we know the darkness of this evil age, we are not *of* the darkness. Living in the present, we nevertheless live as children of tomorrow, as children of hope. Our lives are now bound up with the destiny of Jesus Christ. This does not mean that we do not have to worry about the future because God is in charge of it. Rather, Lehmann's ethic demonstrates that because we have hope in the promises of God's future, which is transfiguring the present age, we parabolically represent that hope which is in us by what we do.

Therefore, one does not motivate Christians to action by activating guilt. While confession of guilt is required for true repentance, guilt itself cripples rather than liberates us to take

38. Alves, *Tomorrow's Child: Imagination, Creativity, and the Rebirth of Culture* (New York: Harper & Row, 1972), p. 194.

action. One also does not motivate Christians to action by activating fear. Constant fear that God's grace will be snatched from us if we do not fulfill the right conditions turns the gospel into a burden. Those who interpret the apocalyptic images of the imminent parousia as the individual's salvation into heaven have also missed the point. Neither the fear of losing the heavenly life nor the hope of achieving it motivates Christian action. The descriptive character of Lehmann's ethic concurs with Pauline apocalyptic that the heavenly life is our given; the context in which we "live and move and have our being" (Acts 17:28) is one that acknowledges the reality of Christ's ultimate victory over the powers and principalities. Our task, according to both the apostle Paul and Paul Lehmann, is to live so that we "image" now the future that is promised in the story of God's action on behalf of creation.

This leads to the second consequence of Paul's image of the Second Coming that is directly consistent with Lehmann's theology: the concept of the Second Coming reinterprets the doctrine of the *imitatio Christi,* the imitation of Christ. Because Pauline ethics is not based on a Platonic ideal by which everything else is judged, human behavior is not compared with the perfect image of Christ that stands always out of our reach. Rather, Paul defines human action by a power which draws that action into its realm. This is consistent with Lehmann's belief that responsible Christian behavior becomes a "fragmentary foretaste" and living parable of the "fulfillment which is already on its way" (*Ethics*). According to Lehmann, we cannot imitate Christ by basing our actions on the teachings of Jesus that have been abstracted from the biblical story of God's dealings with the world in Jesus Christ. Christ is not an ideal or principle but the living Lord who draws us into a new orbit of power.

Lehmann therefore reinterprets the imitation of Christ to mean that our actions become living parables of divine action. Our actions point to the humanizing activity of God in the same way that Jesus' parables pointed to God's graceful movement on behalf of creation. Christian action thus has symbolic significance:

148

> The Christian character of behavior is defined not by the principal parts of an act but by the functional significance of action in the context of the divine economy and of the actuality of the new humanity. Thus behavior, as Christianity understands it, is not qualitatively but symbolically significant. Or, to put the point in the light of Jesus' characteristic mode of teaching, behavior is ethically defined not by perfections but by parabolic power. (*Ethics*, p. 122)

It is not the case, as is often charged, that Lehmann's description of responsible Christian behavior offers no concrete guidance for ethical decisions. While Lehmann does not arm us with universal principles or laws, he does not send us into each situation empty-handed. Whatever the particular context in which we are called upon to act, we always stand in the broader context of the story of God's activity, which has inaugurated the new humanity in this world. Responsible behavior is defined not solely in the context of the particular situation but always also in the context of God's action in Jesus Christ.

To conclude this discussion of the significance of apocalyptic for Lehmann's ethics, it will be helpful to take a brief look at the work of John Dominique Crossan on parable, which will illuminate how the use of story and apocalyptic discussed here coincide to inform what we have just described as parabolic action. John Dominique Crossan's description of the function of parable in opposition to myth will illuminate Lehmann's understanding of the symbolic nature of responsible human action in light of what has already been said about story, apocalyptic, and the action of God.

According to Crossan, myth functions to mediate between irreconcilable opposites in any given situation, whereas parable functions to create irreconciliation. Crossan, relying on the work of Frank Kermode, describes myths as "agents of stability" and parables as "agents of change."[39]

---

39. Crossan, *The Dark Interval: Towards a Theology of Story* (Niles, Ill.: Argus Communications, 1975), pp. 51, 55-56. (All subsequent references

Crossan argues that "there is in every parabolic situation a battle of basic structures." Initially the structural difference lies between what the listener to a story expects to hear and what the teller of a story actually says (*Interval*, p. 66). For instance, the stories of Ruth and Jonah both serve functionally as parables because of this stark contrast between what the listener expects and what the storyteller says:

> Ruth: The hearer expects that God will grant approval to a Jewish-Jewish marriage and disapproval to a Jewish-Foreign one, but the story tells of divine approval to a Jewish-Foreign union. (*Interval*, p. 72)

> Jonah: The hearer expects prophets to obey God, and pagans such as the Ninevites, especially, to disobey God. But the speaker tells a story in which a prophet disobeys and the Ninevites obey beyond all belief. (*Interval*, p. 76)

What is displayed in this battle of structures, however, is not simply the wisdom of a skilled storyteller who takes a listener by surprise. In that case parables would simply function the way an O. Henry story does. The surprise ending would delight the reader but wouldn't necessarily change the reader's understanding of reality. The parabolic presentation of a battle between structures, however, actually changes our world and the way we perceive it by raising the theological question "What if God does not play the game by our rules?" (*Interval*, p. 77). Crossan illustrates the power of this question by referring to Franz Kafka's parable called "Before the Law."

In Kafka's story, a man stands before a door guarded by a doorkeeper. All his life he seeks entrance, and all his life his efforts are thwarted by the doorkeeper. Finally, as he lies dying, he asks

---

to this volume will be made parenthetically in the text.) According to Crossan, "The basic thesis of this book [is] that parable is a story which is the polar, or binary, opposite of myth. Parable brings not peace but the sword, and parable casts fire upon the earth which receives it" (p. 55).

the doorkeeper why in all these years no one else has sought entrance to the Law. The doorkeeper replies that this door was built for this man only: it was for his entrance alone. "And now," concludes the doorkeeper, "I am going to shut it" (*Interval*, p. 78). The idea behind Kafka's skillful structural battle is frighteningly clear: "What if life were like a door intended for you alone but through which you could not enter?" (*Interval*, p. 80).

As Crossan points out, Kafka's parable demonstrates that the function of a parable is not simply to startle a listener in the way an O. Henry story does but to call his or her fundamental understanding of existence into question:

> How exactly can one tell a story which attacks and undermines the hearer's structure of expectation without the hearer simply shrugging off the attack by stating that one's parabolic story just could not happen? It is in the surface structure and texture that the parabler must use consummate skill so that the deep structure of the parable gets into the hearer's consciousness and is only felt in its full force there when it is too late to do much about it. (*Interval*, p. 86)

Crossan's description of parable and Lehmann's description of divine activity here coincide. The stories of the Bible serve this parabolic function of defining reality contrary to our usual way of perceiving it. We are drawn into the world of the biblical story in such a way that the human story and the divine story collide. According to Lehmann, at this point we experience a "saving" story that demands our active participation.

Consistent with Lehmann's ethics, Crossan moves from spoken and written parables to what he calls "parables of *deed*":

> Parables give God room. The parables of Jesus are not historical allegories telling us how God acts with mankind; neither are they moral example-stories telling us how to act before God and towards one another. They are stories which shatter the deep structure of our accepted world and thereby render clear and evident to us the relativity of story itself. They remove our

defenses and make us vulnerable to God. It is only in such experiences that God can touch us, and only in such moments does the kingdom of God arrive. My own term for this relationship is transcendence. (*Interval*, p. 89)

Lehmann's term for this relationship would be not only "transcendence" but also "transfiguration." According to Lehmann, the experience produced by the parabolic battle between structures is not itself the transcendent. It is, however, God's revelation through which the world is transfigured. What we are to do as believers in Jesus Christ and members of his church is to "image" this action — that is, to participate in this transfiguration.

The politics of God demands that our actions parabolically point to the radical discontinuity between God's action and the status quo, to the lordship of Christ over all creation, to the humanizing space created by the inbreaking of the New Age, and to the promised reconciliation among peoples. Such symbolic action makes that reconciliation a present reality.

Given this symbolic character of action, a critical question arises: Can Lehmann's ethics claim accountability in the public arena of ideas? If one relies on biblical images, stories, and concepts to describe the action of God, does ethics become strictly sectarian, with no word to speak to the world? An examination of this issue will conclude our exploration of Lehmann's ethics.

V

Public Accountability and Revolutionary Violence

Public Accountability: A Contemporary Debate

Recently a debate has arisen in Christian ethics over the issue of "public accountability." Those on one side of the issue agree with Robin Lovin that "ethics in the modern world is fundamentally a discipline of giving public reasons for action."[1] These theologians think that Christian ethics must render its arguments accessible to public debate and persuasion. The task of ethics lies in offering people choices, in presenting moral arguments in such a way that others must either agree with us or reject our position. Ethics cannot simply state preferences or declare intentions; it must seek to persuade. Lovin points out that giving theological reasons for ethical decisions may *explain* our behavior but does not provide persuasive arguments in the "public arena" of ideas outside the community that generates and shares such language. Hence Lovin's goal is to establish a "public theology" (*Christian Faith*, p. 3).

---

1. Lovin, *Christian Faith and Public Choices: The Social Ethics of Barth, Brunner, and Bonhoeffer* (Philadelphia: Fortress Press, 1984), p. 2. All subsequent references to this volume will be made parenthetically in the text.

In the works of Karl Barth, Emil Brunner, and Dietrich Bonhoeffer, Lovin discovers two different approaches to Christian ethics and public choices. Whereas all three theologians rejected the identification of a "point of contact" between culture and revelation, Lovin believes that Barth alone took this rejection to its most radical conclusion. Brunner and Bonhoeffer, though different in many respects, approached the relationship between Christian ethics and public social issues with due regard to their interrelation. According to Lovin, Brunner's "orders of creation" and Bonhoeffer's "divine mandates" allowed Christian ethics to live in partnership with the beliefs of those who do not share the Christian faith. Lovin dubs their approach "theological realism," which understands that "Christian ethics is more than, but not other than, the functional requirements of a society in which human life can flourish" (*Christian Faith,* p. 161).

What Lovin means by "more than, but not other than" is not self-evident; furthermore, his claim that both Brunner's and Bonhoeffer's ideas "converge with the main current of modern Catholic thought on natural law" is debatable. Nevertheless, he is correct in describing Barth as unquestionably opposed to any reconciliation between "cultural norms and Christian obedience" (*Christian Faith,* p. 161). Barth emphasized the gulf between the Gospel and "common morality." Lovin dubs Barth's approach to Christian ethics and public choices "theological radicalism."

According to Lovin, by emphasizing the gap between Christian ethics and "common morality," those who follow Barth's more radical line of thought also emphasize the distinctive quality of Christian ethics.[2] This so-called "radical" approach to

2. Lovin says, "The aim of ethics in this theology is, as Stanley Hauerwas puts it, 'to reassert the significance of the church as a distinct society with an integrity peculiar to itself.' The community of faith must not be confused with those institutions [groups that serve the identifiable social functions of education, public order, and economic productivity], must not become another order or mandate alongside them. The lines of discipleship lead in their own directions, and as often as not these will run opposite to what the world requires to maintain order, achieve prosperity, and secure happiness" (*Christian Faith and Public Choices,* p. 162).

theology refuses to establish a common standard such as natural law that both Christians and those of other faiths could agree to embrace. Those who hold this position rely on Christian doctrine as the foundation of ethics rather than a rational ethic common to all reasonable persons, as Lovin explains:

> Here the natural law tension between a universal norm and a concrete situation is replaced by an eschatological tension between humanity transformed by God and the present human condition, and this tension is heightened by the experience of the beginnings of that transformation through membership in the Christian community. (*Christian Faith,* p. 163)

In the current debate over "public accountability," theologians who, like Barth, share this "radical" approach are often criticized for being sectarian. While Lovin says he refuses to level this accusation, others do charge that theologians such as Paul Lehmann and Stanley Hauerwas maintain the distinctiveness of Christian ethics at the cost of the church's responsible involvement in society.

According to Lovin, theological radicalism makes one unwilling to "take sides on less than ultimate issues." For example, he believes that Barth's insistence that Christianity not be confused with any particular cultural or political endeavor made it nearly impossible for Barth to exclude Christians from any side of a political issue. Believing Barth's opposition to Nazism was an exception, Lovin points to Barth's refusal to criticize the Communist takeover of Hungary as an example of his inability to take sides. Lovin claims that "Christian realists" are much more willing to argue "for specific choices that are far less momentous than the issue between East and West that Barth thought faith should leave alone" (*Christian Faith,* pp. 172-73).

But here Lovin has overstated his case, misrepresenting Barth's position and thus misrepresenting those who follow in the tradition of Barth. There was *no* political issue that Barth believed "faith should leave alone." Like the "realists," Barth spoke of "specific choices" on such issues as euthanasia, war, abortion, and so on.[3] If Barth did not make clear choices about specific issues of public significance, one wonders what his discussions are presumed to be about.

Furthermore, even though Barth rejected natural theology, he *did* believe that Christian language must be translated into language understandable to others if the church is to fulfill the "public responsibility of faith."[4] On the one hand, Barth says the church has and must speak its own language — that is, the language of the Bible and of Christian tradition (*Dogmatics*, p. 31). On the other hand, Barth says that "faith necessarily stipulates definite worldly attitudes" which demand the translation of Christian language into language understandable to those outside the church (*Dogmatics*, p. 32):

> Where confession is serious and clear, it must be fundamentally translatable into the speech of Mr. Everyman, the man and woman in the street, into the language of those who are not accustomed to reading Scripture and singing hymns, but who possess a quite different vocabulary and quite different spheres of interest. . . .
>
> By the very nature of the Christian Church there is only one task, to make the Confession heard in the sphere of the world as well. Not now repeated in the language of Canaan, but in the quite sober, quite unedifying language which is spoken out there. There must be translation, for example, into the language of the newspaper. What we have to do is to say in the common language of the world the same thing as we say in the forms of Church language. . . . We know this language of the pulpit and the altar, which outside the area of the church is as effectual as Chinese. Let us beware of remaining stuck where we are and refusing to advance to meet worldly attitudes. (Ibid., pp. 32-33)

3. See Barth, *Church Dogmatics,* 4 vols., trans. Geoffrey Bromiley (Edinburgh: T. & T. Clark, 1936-69), 3/4.

4. Barth, *Church Dogmatics in Outline,* trans. G. T. Thomson (London: SCM Press, 1949), p. 30. All subsequent references to this volume will be made parenthetically in the text.

"May we be confronted . . . with the fact that what has to happen in the Church must go out into the form of worldly attitudes" (ibid., p. 33). These are words from the same Karl Barth whose theological method begins with revelation, not culture, and who rejects all forms of natural theology. For Barth, it is not natural theology but the power of the Holy Spirit that makes such translation possible.

The work of Stanley Hauerwas shares some theological tenets with Barth's work and can be described in Lovin's terms as a "radical approach." Similar to Barth, Hauerwas disagrees with the assumption that "theological ethics must develop arguments that should compel consent from all rational subjects, irrespective of their religious convictions." According to Hauerwas, this assumption puts Christian ethicists in the odd position of claiming that Christian moral convictions have little or no relation to Christian theological convictions. The Christian ethicist has nothing different to say than "what any right-thinking person or moral philosopher would say."[5]

Hauerwas believes that the claims for such common moral agreement founded on rational argument are fraught with problems:

> Such agreement can be maintained only by providing an account of morality so formal that it cannot possibly have any normative implications. In fact I take the moral challenge of our time to be the recognition that we live amid "fragments" of past moral positions, none of which can claim our loyalty on grounds of rationality in itself. In such a situation, by taking seriously the particularity of Christian convictions perhaps I can at least help clarify the difficulty of formulating public policy where it involves moral issues.[6]

5. Hauerwas, "Theological Reflection on *In Vitro* Fertilization," in *Suffering Presence: Theological Reflections on Medicine, the Mentally Handicapped, and the Church* (Notre Dame: University of Notre Dame Press, 1986), p. 142.

6. Ibid., p. 143.

Hauerwas claims that the "primary function of religious belief is not to describe the world or to determine the rightness or wrongness of particular actions, but to form a community that understands itself as having a particular mission in the world."[7]

Hauerwas's arguments are not without appeal to logic. The difference between Hauerwas's approach and Lovin's approach is that Hauerwas does not identify logic as an autonomous arena where one can establish commonality with those outside the community. While one's logic may indeed appeal to someone outside the faith, its aim is not to create a common ground. Lovin, on the other hand, identifies "middle axioms" as providing the "common ground" that ethics in the tradition of Karl Barth rejects.

Lehmann: Against a Double Standard. Lehmann's work anticipated this debate regarding public accountability some twenty years ago. Lehmann, however, identified it as the problem of the "double standard," one of the most critical problems, he believed, of Christian ethics:

> The crucial problem of Christian ethics in the context of the
> *koinonia* is how the behavior of Christians is to be related to the
> behavior of non-Christians. How can a *koinonia* ethic make any
> ethical claims upon those in society who do not acknowledge

---

7. Ibid. An example of how Hauerwas puts that primary function into effect lies in his response to the issue of *in vitro* fertilization. Hauerwas does not set out to demonstrate on strictly logical grounds why *in vitro* fertilization should or should not be permitted. Rather, he sets out to demonstrate how Christians making a decision on this issue must be consistent with the Christian understanding of the kind of community the church is and what attitudes are appropriate to that community, in this case stressing the particular importance of attitudes regarding "parenting." In this way Hauerwas shifts the identification of what is ethically significant from the particular act to the agent and to the community to which the agent belongs: "It is not a question of whether *in vitro* fertilization is right or wrong, but a practical judgment of whether this kind of technique furthers or is compatible with our community's understanding of itself." Ethical decisions, therefore, have primarily to do not with the rightness or wrongness of a particular act but with the identity (character) of the person or persons doing the action.

the *koinonia* as their point of departure and frankly live neither in it nor by its light? Do we have here a kind of double ethical standard: one for Christians and another for non-Christians?[8]

Lehmann considers this issue serious enough to threaten his whole approach to ethics. Before turning to his proposal, it is important to examine four responses that he rejects. These are (1) the way of conformity by conscription, (2) the way of conformity by accommodation, (3) natural law, and (4) middle axioms. Clearly Lehmann's designations for the first two "ways" are highly value-laden. No one sets out to write a "theology of conscription" or a "theology of accommodation." This does not mean, however, that Lehmann is merely battling straw opponents. Although theologians may not consciously propose such approaches, some forms of theology can result in these errors.

"Conformity by conscription," on the one hand, insists that non-Christians conform to the behavioral standards defined by the church. In this scheme of things a religiously plural society is forced to live by the standards of the single most powerful form of religion. This attempt at conformity carries an ever-present danger to the relation between church and state. According to Lehmann, a *koinonia* ethic, with its emphasis on the humanizing activity of God and its understanding of the function of law, will not allow "prescriptive conformity in the name of religious faith" (*Ethics,* p. 146). Lehmann claims that law serves divine activity by exposing the boundary between human and inhuman acts. If a law does not perform this function, the Christian does not count it as law. To insist that civil law be made to conform to religious convictions is untenable in light of this humanizing activity of God: "The inability to compel ethical behavior is part of the economy of God, whereby . . . human wholeness may be served but is never achieved by law" (*Ethics,* pp. 146-47).

8. Lehmann, *Ethics in a Christian Context* (New York: Harper & Row, 1963), p. 145. All subsequent references to this volume will be made parenthetically in the text.

"Conformity through accommodation," on the other hand, means that the church does not compel conformity to its own standards but accepts the standards of the culture as its own. According to this approach, no common ground has to be sought between the morality of the church and the morality of society, because there is no radical distinction between them (*Ethics*, p. 147).

Lehmann warns against the errors of these two alternatives: "The way of conformity alienates the non-Christian and divides the religious community itself. The way of accommodation ignores or betrays the dynamics and direction of a *koinonia* ethos" (*Ethics*, p. 147).

Lehmann also rejects natural law as a way to avoid a double standard. Proponents of natural law believe that "there is a common link between the believer and the nonbeliever grounded in the nature of the human reason" (*Ethics*, p. 147). This common link allows believer and nonbeliever to come to agreement on certain ethical judgments. This is the position argued for by Robin Lovin, a position Lehmann describes this way: "Natural law claims that the human intellect discerns the reciprocity between ethical reality and human reality as self-evident, whether or not the ability of discernment is a result of divine implantation or natural capacity."[9] Not least among Lehmann's reasons for rejecting natural law is that the doctrine of human sin will not allow for any suggestion of a natural capacity to discern the good. He believes that certain Christian presuppositions necessitate the rejection of natural law. These presuppositions become clear when one examines four things:

9. Lehmann, "A Christian Alternative to Natural Law," in *Die moderne Demokratie und Ihr Recht: Festschrift für Gerhard Leibholz* first ed., ed. Karl Dietrich Bracher et al. (Tübingen: J. C. B. Mohr [Paul Siebeck], 1966), p. 531. In his *Ethics in a Christian Context* Lehmann rejected this alternative without fully addressing it. He promised a further discussion of the issue of natural law in a subsequent volume. While that volume has not yet been published, Lehmann has addressed the issue in the article cited here. All subsequent references to this article will be made parenthetically in the text.

(1) in what sense one speaks of natural law, (2) in what sense one refers to an "alternative" to natural law, (3) in what sense one uses the adjective "Christian," and (4) how one interprets the concept of sovereignty.[10]

First, Lehmann says, natural law refers to the claim that human reason has the natural capacity to identify the right or the good. Thus the philosopher Cicero defined natural law as "the highest reason, implanted in nature, which commands what things are to be done, and which forbids the contrary."[11] Over time Christian theologians began to appropriate natural law for Christianity. For instance, a thousand years after Cicero, Philipp Melanchthon claimed that "natural law is the common judgment to which all men alike assent, which God has engraved upon the mind of each, and which is designed to fashion morals."[12] Hence, while natural law is not a notion generated originally by Christians, one aspect of the Christian tradition has claimed that God is the author of natural law. Through it, God's will is put into action.

The second presupposition involves the sense in which one refers to an "alternative" to natural law. According to Lehmann, proponents of natural law fear that any alternative will lead to ethical relativism or even nihilism and, therefore, to the break-down of morality.[13] As one who stands among the critics of

10. This last presupposition rules the other three. Just as the question of sovereignty governed the debate between nineteenth-century liberalism and twentieth-century dialectical theology, so it governs here. Natural law moves theology in the direction of transferring sovereignty from God to the people ("A Christian Alternative to Natural Law," p. 538).

11. "A Christian Alternative to Natural Law," p. 521. Lehmann is quoting Cicero, *De legibus*, 1.6.18: *"Lex est ratio summa, insita in natura, quae iubet ea, quae facienda sunt, prohibet que contraria."*

12. Lehmann is quoting Melanchthon, *On Christian Doctrine: Loci communes*, trans. and ed. Clyde Manschreck (New York: Oxford University Press, 1965).

13. Lehmann easily dismisses the concern that each side has exaggerated its characterization of the errors of the other. He apparently accepts this as a usual aspect of ethical debate: "The *ad hominem* consideration that both exponents and critics of the natural law tradition have sometimes overstated the case may be regarded as an obvious datum of the story of

161

natural law, Lehmann wants to take seriously the danger of falling into ethical relativism:

> We are insistently concerned about the intrinsic connection between the responsible life and an order of ethical certainty and guidance which has so steadily and unyieldingly marked the adherence to natural law. Conversely, we are fully aware of, and have no wish to court, the perils of thorough-going ethical relativism. ("Christian Alternative," p. 523)

Lehmann seeks to uncover an alternative to natural law that provides something other than either strict rational certainty or ethical relativism. He believes this provision can occur only through an *alternative* to, not a revision of, natural law. Such an alternative is demanded by an "internal flaw" and an "external oversight" that make natural law unacceptable to the Christian faith ("Christian Alternative," p. 524).

The "internal flaw" lies in the fact that human reason "cannot bear the normative weight assigned to it" by natural law theory ("Christian Alternative," p. 531). Natural law claims that the reciprocity between ethical reality and human ability is self-evident to human reason. According to Lehmann, human reason simply cannot fulfill such a claim, whether such ability results from divine implantation or natural capacity.

The "external oversight" has to do with the relation of biblical authority to natural law. A system of natural law forces scriptural authority into a supplemental role. If the Bible is thoroughly compatible with the truth and ethics of philosophy, then the Bible becomes nothing more than a "marginal corrective" or "complementary addendum" ("Christian Alternative," p. 532). In keeping with his understanding of revelation, Lehmann asserts that Scripture has a catalytic rather than a supplementary function. The content of Scripture reverses the order of secular wisdom. These reversals mean "that biblical premises

---

ethical reflection, without pertinence to the present purpose" ("A Christian Alternative to Natural Law," p. 523).

transvalue rather than correct or complete the self-understanding of a culture or of man in his culture" ("Christian Alternative," p. 533).

As mentioned, Christian theologians sought to appropriate the classical understanding of natural law by claiming that natural law was created by God. God, as the author of reason, demands that we follow the dictates of reason as laid down in natural law. Lehmann believes, however, that Aquinas and others who made this move were simply seeking to say the same things the philosophers were saying, only in a different way, rather than making distinctively Christian claims. Accordingly, Christian natural law is not a "Christian alternative" to philosophical interpretations of natural law at all. It is simply a "Christianized version" of a natural law theory that was already formulated.

Lehmann's final presupposition has to do with the concept of sovereignty. Some critics of natural law claim that in a "world come of age," the usefulness of ethical absolutism has come to an end. Lehmann agrees that if there is no other function for God than "that of chief bailiff, issuing restraining orders and supervising the serving process until the 'moral law within' (Kant) catches up with 'the moral fuss within and without' (Freud)," then "God is indeed expendable" ("Christian Alternative," p. 526).

Nevertheless, while agreeing that the "long minority of humanity is at an end" (to use Comte's phrase), Lehmann believes that maturity is not as easily acquired as some philosophers have proposed ("Christian Alternative," p. 526). As pointed out in the last chapter, Lehmann believes that maturity and humanization require not the abandonment of transcendence but a new interpretation of the relationship between a transcendent authority and humanity. Natural law claims to subordinate human will to human reason. Lehmann claims, however, that this transfer of sovereignty from will to reason fails.

Just as the Bible becomes supplemental, the significance of Christ is diminished when interpreted in the context of natural law theory ("Christian Alternative," p. 533). Like Reinhold Niebuhr, Lehmann believes that Christ discloses the divine purpose, a purpose that both occurs within history and governs history ("Christian Alternative," p. 534).[14] According to Lehmann, natural theology's shift from history to reason is a "messianic error" that destroys sovereignty. Jesus of Nazareth, identified as the Christ, provides a "humanizing transcendence" that natural theology cannot sustain.

In addition to rejecting conformity through conscription or through accommodation and natural law, Lehmann also rejects "middle axioms" as the avenue for providing common moral ground between Christians and non-Christians. This, of course, sets Lehmann, like Hauerwas, in direct opposition to Lovin, who advocates the use of middle axioms as a way to formulate public theology.

According to Lovin, the so-called "Christian realist" provides the generality required for public moral discourse by expressing the basic values of the faith in terms like "justice," "freedom," and "equality," which can be understood and argued by all, and by linking those values to specific claims about what, under present conditions, must be done to realize them in society. J. H. Oldham christened these imperatives "middle axioms"(*Christian Faith*, p. 173).[15] Whereas middle axioms can help determine policy, they are not identical with specific policy. Consequently, Christians can comment on the general direction of a policy without dictating their views into law. Middle axioms

14. Here Lehmann refers to Reinhold Niebuhr, *The Nature and Destiny of Man,* vol. 2 (New York: Charles Scribner's Sons, 1943), pp. 4-5.

15. Lovin's reference is to J. H. Oldham, "The Function of the Church in Society," in W. A. Visser 't Hooft and J. H. Oldham, *The Church and Its Function in Society* (Chicago: Willett-Clark, 1937), p. 210. Lehmann, however, responded to John C. Bennett's argument for middle axioms in a lecture entitled "Principles and the Situation" presented at the January 1958 meeting of the Society of Professors of Christian Ethics and Social Ethics. See John C. Bennett, *Storm Over Ethics* (Philadelphia: United Church Press, 1967) and *Christian Ethics and Social Policy* (New York: Charles Scribner's Sons, 1946), pp. 77-83. See also Ronald Preston, "Middle Axioms," in *The Westminster Dictionary of Christian Ethics,* rev. ed., ed. James F. Childress and John Macquarrie (Philadelphia: Westminster Press, 1986), p. 382.

are "middle" because they fall "in between" universal principles and the particular ethical situation. They are "axioms" rather than principles because they make no claim to universality (*Ethics,* p. 151).[16] Middle axioms, therefore, provide that common ground which produces the public accountability sought by ethicists such as Robin Lovin.

According to John C. Bennett, middle axioms express moral convictions that are common both to Christians and to non-Christians. He uses desegregation as an example of a "middle axiom." Here the absolute principle is Christian love, while the concrete situation is racial injustice. "In between" the absolute and the specific situation is desegregation, the instrument or "middle axiom" whereby Christian love is brought to bear upon racial injustice. A non-Christian may not care about Christian love but can join the Christian in pressing for desegregation. Thus the middle axiom provides common ethical ground where Christians and non-Christians can meet.

While Lehmann's *koinonia* ethic leads him to agree with Bennett's stance on desegregation, it leads him to a different identification of what is ethical in this situation (*Ethics,* pp. 151-52). Lehmann pronounces "ethically unreal" any attempt to clarify or justify the application of principles to concrete situations, for this "logical enterprise" cannot close the gap between the abstract principle and the specific situation. Lehmann believes that the focus is shifted from "logic to life" when one claims that what is ethically significant in any situation is the "humanizing action of God" (*Ethics,* p. 153). By shifting the focus from "logic" to "life," Lehmann intends to emphasize the task of ethics as describing and analyzing the context in which human life is nourished and brought to human wholeness. For Christians, God's revelation in Jesus Christ sets the boundaries for that human wholeness. Desegregation becomes a "sign" of

16. Lehmann claims that "the important concern connoted by 'middle axioms' is that there be some designation of objectives or judgments which have a particular reference to our concrete situation, which are determiners of policy and yet not identical with the most concrete policy guiding an immediate action" (*Ethics in a Christian Context,* p. 148).

God's activity on behalf of human maturity. A situation takes on ethical significance not from the attempt to formulate and apply ethical principles but from "what God is doing in the world to make and to keep human life human" (*Ethics,* p. 152).

The difference between Lehmann's position and Bennett's position lies in the question of whether there is a "self-validating" connection between reason and the highest good. Bennett charges Lehmann with establishing his position exclusively on theological considerations and thereby robbing it of "public" force.[17] He claims that there must be broader principles that allow the Christian to converse with the non-Christian. Accordingly, Bennett brings us back to a "gentle" natural theology. Lehmann believes that in so doing Bennett loses what is distinctively Christian. Once moral convictions are given a "broader base than Christian revelation," that which is distinctively Christian becomes expendable (*Ethics,* p. 149).

Both Lehmann and Bennett argue in favor of desegregation as a way to fight racist "separate-but-equal" practices. They differ, however, on why and how one arrives at that decision. In Bennett's case, what is ethically significant about the situation is "provided by a rational principle." In Lehmann's case, the "ethical factor" is identified by the "sign character of the behavior." Lehmann summarizes his viewpoint by saying, "In short, desegregation is ethical in so far as it is a sign of the new humanity which is coming to be in the world in which Jesus Christ lived and died, over which he rules as Lord against the day of his coming again" (*Ethics,* p. 152).

Lehmann claims that middle axioms are ethically expendable — not Christian wisdom that arises from divine revelation (*Ethics,* p. 154).

Lehmann sees Bennett's concept of "middle axioms" as simply a "vestigial remnant" of the tradition of natural law. Grounded in theological anthropology, such a tradition cannot, according to Lehmann, sustain Christian ethical reflection. Instead, he insists that Christian theological ethics must have a

17. Lovin makes the same charge against Karl Barth.

firm Christological foundation. "A theology of messianism according to which behavior is the parabolic bearer of new humanity intrinsically connects both 'gospel' and 'situation' and also the behavior of unbelievers with that of believers" (*Ethics,* p. 154). Lehmann's alternative to natural law and his response to the question of public accountability will always have a Christological rather than an autonomously rational foundation.

Having rejected these four ways (conscription, accommodation, natural law, and middle axioms), Lehmann proposes several alternatives for relating believer and nonbeliever. The first alternative points to the sign character of Christian action. As discussed in the last chapter, Christian ethics, according to Lehmann, interprets actions as signs of what God is doing in the world. For instance, Lehmann claims that "desegregation is ethically significant because it points to what God is doing in the world to achieve the humanization of man." If Christians and non-Christians find themselves working together to bring about desegregation, this is a sign that they stand on common ethical ground. That common ground, however, is not identified by Christians as a common rationality between them and non-Christians. Rather, Christians claim that what is common between them is the humanizing action of God, which includes all humanity, not just Christians.

Second, the common ground between believer and nonbeliever is not common rational persuasion but the "common ethical predicament" that causes each to ask questions regarding true humanity and human maturity. Lehmann translates the question "What shall I do to be saved?" as one that reflects this predicament. This question can be expressed not only by asking "How do I get into heaven?" as a Christian tends to put it, but also by asking, "What can I do to be who I am?" as a non-Christian tends to put it. Although Christian and non-Christian are here speaking a different "language," both, according to Lehmann, are asking the same thing. It is not necessary for one to use the language of the other.

Third, the biblical tradition itself claims that the divine economy includes those outside the Christian faith. Jesus has "other sheep, that are not of this fold" (*Ethics*, p. 159). Lehmann believes that relating believer and unbeliever through natural theology results in a "sterile discussion of the relations between natural and revealed theology, of the image of God and of how much of it remains untarnished by sin, of formal and material humanity" (*Ethics*, p. 158). He suggests instead that we turn to the notion of the "general power of the Spirit":

> The general power of the Spirit provides the kind of theological and ethical substance and sobriety which intrinsically links the divine economy with human maturity and puts believers and unbelievers upon a common level of integrity about what the struggle for human maturity involves, and upon a common level of imaginative discernment about what the secret of maturity is. (*Ethics*, p. 158)

The unbeliever and the believer do not arrive at the same conclusion on an ethical issue because they share a common natural capacity to do the good. Rather, they can come to the same conclusion because each is led by the power of the Holy Spirit. A *koinonia* ethic can resolve the problem of the double standard by "including nonbelievers among the other sheep of the Holy Spirit of God." As Lehmann explains, "The same spirit which informs the *koinonia* informs also the shaping of the new humanity in the world" (*Ethics*, p. 158).

Natural law sought to shift the focus of ethics from divine will to human reason. In the process it lost a sense of humanizing transcendence — that is, the sovereignty of God. Lehmann's alternative to natural law, which describes a "messianic criticism" of religion, completely contradicts the public theology sought by scholars such as Lovin:

> The fruits of this messianic criticism are a perspective and a power to shape the judgments and actions of men in the enterprise of humanization. . . . In the light of such a perspective and power, the natural law has been displaced by an order of providence in which the will of man is directed towards the redeeming of the times, the reason toward the discernment of

the times, and law bends the things which have been towards the things which are to come. ("Christian Alternative," p. 535)

To displace natural law with "an order of providence" certainly does not land us in the public arena. Lehmann still employs the images of faith: providence, redemption, eschatology. How does this lead to a responsible reply to the serious question of the double standard?

Lehmann describes the Christian alternative to natural law in the following way:

A genuine Christian alternative to natural law would be a descriptive analysis of the intrinsic and inviolable reciprocity between the responsible life and human life, a reciprocity anchored, not in the human reason, with or without divine assistance, but in a perspective upon the foundations and directives for the making of decisions, whether private or public, derived from the insights and sensitivity nourished by Christian faith, Christian thought, and Christian experience. ("Christian Alternative," p. 526)

In other words, while the reciprocity between ethical reality and human reality is intrinsic to Christian faith, natural law has no such intrinsic relation to Christianity. Because Christianity is concerned with that which is human, it is concerned about humanization for all persons, not just Christians.

According to Lehmann, God's action is identified anywhere humanizing activity takes place. This does not mean that humanization is a universal concept that may or may not take on Christian meaning. For Lehmann, humanization is defined by God's activity in Jesus Christ. That there are those outside the Christian faith who make the same claims or advocate the same actions for the purpose of furthering humanization is as much a product of the workings of the Holy Spirit as Christian claims and actions are. Lehmann will not define humanization apart from the use of Christian words. He does, however, readily acknowledge that others outside the Christian faith can and do employ such definitions.

Lehmann is not only concerned with Christians' relationship with those outside the Christian faith in terms of the issue of public accountability. His work also reflects concern for Christian attitudes about those outside the faith in general. While Lehmann does not concede the particularity and uniqueness of the Christian faith in the face of today's concern over pluralism, he does care whether Christians include other people within the purview of God's encompassing providential care.

At the heart of Lehmann's understanding of the relationship between Christians and non-Christians is a clear but unspoken allegiance to universal salvation. As this discussion has unfolded, various aspects of Lehmann's thought have raised the issue of the relationship between the church and those outside the church. At each juncture, Lehmann's work points to the inclusive activity of the Holy Spirit.

If, for instance, one believes that God's action in Jesus Christ is what makes us truly human, then what of those who do not acknowledge Christ? If the Christian story is a saving story of the presence of transcendence, must we foreswear the stories of other faiths? If we believe Christ is the sole Lord of the world, what do we say about those who do not acknowledge the lordship of Christ? Lehmann's concepts of maturity, story, lordship, and the New Age all demonstrate his affirmation of the inclusive activity of the Spirit.

Maturity. Lehmann's understanding of maturity as the product of God's action in Jesus Christ sets the context for how "mature" Christians relate to those outside their community of faith. Against Christian maturity, which is a product of God's humanizing activity, he contrasts the "pathological immaturity" that sometimes characterizes the church's tendency to move within the "unholy and unhealthy rhythm of dogmatism and pietism":

According to this rhythm, a believer is never willing to take his fellow man, whether believer or unbeliever, as he is, but always wants to impose upon his fellow, as a precondition of their fellowship, the doctrinal pattern of his own belief. And when this attack upon the integrity of the other succumbs to the enervating futility of rational formulations, the other side of the coin presently turns face up. The believer then gets emotional about his faith, as though the *koinonia* could be authenticated by internalization. ("Christian Alternative," p. 526)

According to Lehmann, true Christian maturity understands that forcing one's doctrinal beliefs on others violates the integrity of the body of Christ to which we belong — that is, violates our "fundamental humanity" Christ restored through the incarnation, cross, and resurrection. Because the *koinonia* is Christ's body in the world, it is called to reflect the "pattern of integrity" established by the interrelatedness between Christ and the community of believers. We understand from Christian maturity that human behavior is not universalized but socialized; mature Christian behavior seeks always to establish human interrelatedness, not uniformity of thought and action (*Ethics*, pp. 54, 56).

Story. Lehmann's concept of story raises the issue of whether Christians alone have access to a "saving" story. Given that he defines a saving story as one that provides an image and an experience of transcendence, does Lehmann believe that the only story which saves is that of the Christian faith? According to Lehmann, the Christian story itself teaches us to answer this question in the negative:

> Too often . . . the [Christian] story has been told as though exclusiveness were the criterion of its particularity. But the contrary is actually the case. The Christian story . . . moves from its divine-human center of freedom and fulfillment to its circumference from which nothing human is excluded.[18]

18. Lehmann, "The Indian Situation as a Question of Accountability," *Church and Society*, Jan./Feb. 1985, p. 59. This essay is an abbreviated version of a lecture entitled "Identity, Difference and Human Community: Some Theological Perspectives Pertinent to Law and the Indian Situation," which was presented for discussion at a symposium entitled "Theology, Jurisprudence and the Indian Situation," held under the auspices of the Division of Church and Society of the National Council of Churches at the

It is not affirmation of a common, universal religious experience that leads Lehmann to acknowledge the existence of other saving stories.[19] Consistent with the Reformed tradition, he believes not in the "essentially religious" nature of human beings but in their "total depravity." Further, unlike those who take a liberal approach, he believes in the uniqueness of the Christian proclamation. The gospel is not simply using different words to say the same thing as every other form of religious thought. Nevertheless, the particular, concrete content of the Christian story includes within it the affirmation of God's concern for *all* humanity. This divine concern coupled with divine freedom does not allow Christians to have a judgmental attitude toward others.[20]

Lehmann agrees with James Cone, who insists that because the gospel sets us in relationship with others, we are called to listen to stories outside the Bible — stories from Africa and Asia, for example. Like Lehmann, Cone does not believe that listening to other stories requires relinquishing or even diminishing one's commitment to the Christian story. In fact, just the opposite is true. Since the Christian story calls us to be defenders of life, Cone says, "faith itself forces one to remain open to life as it is lived anywhere." When being "open to life" is understood as humanization and liberation, Cone and Lehmann stand together in believing that a willingness to listen to the stories of other faiths arises from the conviction that our own faith "is the defender of life."

Christ's Lordship. In recent years feminist theology has rightly claimed that the church too often believes that the concept of Christ's lordship over us permits a parallel human structure whereby some individuals exercise lordship over others — for example, Christians over non-Christians, men over women,

---

Center for Continuing Education in Princeton, New Jersey, December 1983.

19. This would be the stance of the experiential-expressivist position.

20. James Cone, *God of the Oppressed* (New York: Seabury Press, 1975), p. 104.

white persons over persons of color. It is true, of course, that this is the stance the church often takes. Affirmation of the lordship of Christ does not, however, justify such a turn. God's action toward us liberates us, enabling us to act like human beings, *not* like gods. The lordship of Christ declares all other claims to lordship illegitimate. God does not call us to be lords over our neighbors because only Jesus Christ is Lord.

New Age/Old Age. Lehmann's use of the image of the New Age inaugurated by Jesus Christ once again leads to the issue of the church's relationship with non-Christian religious bodies. If God's invasion into the world creates a new space in which we live, does it follow that all who do not live within that space defined as the Christian *koinonia* are condemned by Christ? Some people are rightly fearful that the war imagery essential to apocalyptic thinking will lead to the image of "Christian soldiers marching off to war" and proclaiming, "If you refuse to live within this new space created by Christ, we will destroy you, or at least we will pronounce you eternally damned." Does apocalyptic by definition lead to the mentality of the Crusades?

Both the apostle Paul and Paul Lehmann answer, "By no means!" If Christ is the defender of life, Lehmann would ask with James Cone, how can we possibly believe that we are called upon to pronounce death and damnation?[21] Our apocalyptic vocation does not lead us to say, "If you refuse to live in this new space, we will destroy you in the name of Christ," but rather, "We will struggle to defy the powers of darkness that seek to destroy and oppress, no matter who the victim is."[22] The battle is not one of Christians against non-Christians. We struggle on behalf of those who are perishing at the hands of the powers and principalities, no matter who those persons might be.

21. Ibid.
22. According to J. Louis Martyn, God is "the Passionate Advocate" of each one of us, and it is this God who calls us "to fight the only good fight in the world" (Martyn, "From Paul to Flannery O'Connor," *Katallagete* 7.4 [Winter 1981]: 17).

In radical distinction from the theology of the apocalypses, the lordship of Christ leads us not to demarcate the "saved" from the "damned" but to affirm that "both believer and unbeliever belong to Christ" (*Ethics*, p. 117). As we read in 1 Corinthians 15:22, "For as in Adam all die, so also in Christ shall *all* be made alive." That Christ is Lord of the world as well as of the church indicates that the church has no room to boast of special privilege. If we seek to lord ourselves over others, we have not accurately answered the ethical question "Who is our Lord?" nor have we yet recognized our apocalyptic vocation, which calls us to live in the New Age inaugurated by Jesus Christ.

Like Karl Barth, Lehmann never uses the term "universalism" to describe his theological position regarding those who live according to other faiths or no faith at all. Nevertheless, his position could be so described. Universal salvation has always been deemed a dangerous concept by the church because it threatens to reduce the gospel to a highly relativistic expression of truth that can make no urgent claim upon us. Identifying Lehmann's position as universalistic, however, does not indicate that he believes it makes no difference what one believes. Lehmann's universal position grows from an affirmation of the freedom of the Holy Spirit to move as God wills and to include all of creation in God's political, humanizing activity.

Lehmann does not set out to write a public theology that will appeal to the reason of Christians and non-Christians alike. Nevertheless, he does believe that God's humanizing activity is for the whole of creation. As Christians seek to participate in actions that will provide signs of God's activity in the world, they do so within the context of the church but on behalf of the world. Lehmann is concerned with accountability but not "public accountability" as defined by Lovin. Lehmann believes we are accountable to God for the creation entrusted to our care. Accordingly, we seek to live in a relationship of reciprocal responsibility to all other creatures of God.

Revolutionary Violence

This examination of the work of Paul Lehmann will conclude with an example of how his method works when he is faced with a particular moral issue: revolutionary violence. The discussion will demonstrate how Lehmann's assessment of the relationship between the Christian faith and revolutionary activity combines the concepts of story, apocalyptic, and parabolic action.

Lehmann's interest in the pertinence of Jesus Christ to revolutionary activity was spawned by the turmoil of the 1960s in this country and elsewhere. He was concerned that society no longer had a "center" that could hold human beings together in mature, humanizing relationships. In place of a center that holds society together, he believed we had either an "empty center," which results in chaos, or a "center" that can hold human society together only through tyrannical order.[23] According to Lehmann, "at the center . . . what is happening and what is required are nothing less than the transfiguration of politics" (*Transfiguration*, p. xiii). Such a transfiguration is one in which the humanizing passion for freedom that calls revolutions into being can be sustained.

Because the late 1960s and the early 1970s in America were a time of revolution, some Christian theologians were bound to employ the discipline of theology in the service of revolutionary jargon, and some critics count Lehmann among them. They charge him with abandoning the Christian message for the prevailing mood of the times, and they find his book on revolution, *The Transfiguration of Politics*, sloganeering.[24] For

23. Lehmann, *The Transfiguration of Politics* (New York: Harper & Row, 1975), p. xi. All subsequent references to this volume will be made parenthetically in the text.

24. See the following book reviews of *The Transfiguration of Politics*: Frederick Sontag, "Christ and Revolution," *The Christian Century*, 1-14 Jan. 1976, pp. 22-23; and Rubem A. Alves, "Bringing about Love," *Interpretation* 30 (Apr. 1976): 196-200. See also the reviews by Stanley Hauerwas, *Worldview* 18 (Dec. 1975): 45-48; James Gustafson, *Theology Today* 32 (July 1975): 197ff.; Richard Rowling, *Horizons* 2 (Fall 1975): 268-69; and Charles West, *Princeton Seminary Bulletin* 68 (Autumn 1975): 100.

Lehmann, however, the apocalyptic character of the action of God demands a recognition that revolutionary activity which challenges the abuses of power by the establishment more nearly signifies God's action than activity that supports the status quo.

It is important to keep in mind that when Lehmann refers to revolution, he does not mean any and all political activity which seeks to overthrow existing governments. "Revolution," he says, refers only to that political activity which seeks "to give human shape to the freedom that being and staying human take" (*Transfiguration,* p. xiii). If a political attempt to overthrow the existing system is not made in order to secure human freedom for all, it may be a revolt or a civil war or a coup, but it is not a revolution.[25]

The subtitle of Lehmann's book, a subtitle that is found only on the book's dust jacket, reads, "The Presence and Power of Jesus of Nazareth in and over Human Affairs." Although "revelation" does not form a distinct category in any of its chapters, this book is essentially about revelation. Lehmann seeks to demonstrate the difference that God's revelation in Jesus Christ makes in an age of revolution (*Transfiguration,* p. xiii). Previously I have pointed out that Lehmann believes revelation refers not only to knowledge but also to the power of God's presence which has broken into the world. Our ability to recognize God's presence comes from our having heard the saving story of God's activity in the world.

Lehmann's argument revolves around the claim that revolutions need a "liberating story" to prevent them from "devouring their own children" — that is, to keep them from succumbing to the same oppressive, tyrannical use of power that they

25. According to Lehmann, "Freedom is at once the root and the fruit, the sign and the seal of revolution, at the level both of happening and of mentality" (*The Transfiguration of Politics,* p. 5). Hannah Arendt points out that the American Revolution was a fight for freedom from tyranny. The French Revolution began as the same but became a fight for freedom from necessity. The latter, therefore, involved the poor in a way that the American Revolution did not.

originally set out to overthrow.[26] He believes that the gospel provides such a liberating story in its account of the life, death, and destiny of Jesus Christ.[27] The "presence of Jesus Christ in human affairs," he says, can save revolutionary promise (that people will be made free) from revolutionary fate (that revolutions will succumb to violence as evil as that which they seek to overthrow).

Drawing on his reading of the works of Hannah Arendt, Lehmann says there are four stories that shed light on the bond between revolution and humanization: (1) the "primal" stories of Cain and Abel and Romulus and Remus, (2) the "ancestral" stories of the Exodus in the Bible and Virgil's Aeneas, (3) the "heroic" story of America's founding fathers, and (4) the "messianic" or saving story of Jesus Christ. Lehmann is concerned with which story lends "integrative force" to the promises and achievements of revolution — in other words, with which story prevents a revolution from becoming a "reign of terror" (*Transfiguration,* p. 11). It is the contrast between the first story (the primal story of Cain and Abel) and the fourth (the messianic story) that illuminates this concern.

The primal story of Cain and Abel indicates that societal beginnings are always rooted in violence. The story tells us that whatever achievements humanity has made in political organization and human community, they always had their origin in crime.[28]

According to Arendt, the connection between political beginnings and violence described in this primal story is given a more chilling account in the contemporary retelling of the story of Cain and Abel. Herman Melville's *Billy Budd* reverses the original story by asking the question "What if Abel killed

26. Lehmann discovered the image of revolutions "devouring their children" in Hannah Arendt's book entitled *On Revolution.*

27. Because of the claims Lehmann makes for the connections between revolution and the gospel in *The Transfiguration of Politics,* this book has spawned an enormous amount of controversy. The most heated disagreement has come from the pacifist Stanley Hauerwas.

28. Arendt, *On Revolution* (New York: Viking Press, 1965), p. 10.

Cain?" Melville's intention in this reversal, according to Arendt, is to ponder these questions: "What if the inherently good person is the one who commits violence? What if goodness is as strong as evil, but as open to violence?"

> Let us suppose that from now on the foundation stone of our political life will be that Abel slew Cain. Don't you see that from this deed of violence the same chain of wrong-doing will follow, only that now mankind will not even have the consolation that the violence it must call crime is indeed characteristic of evil men only?[29]

In yet another retelling of the Cain and Abel story, this time in *Demian* by Hermann Hesse, Lehmann believes that the metaphor linking violence with political beginnings takes another step from being necessary (Cain and Abel), to being justified (*Billy Budd*), to being glorified (*Demian*). If this is the story that gives identity to revolution, then revolution and humanization are torn apart; revolution becomes the reign of terror.

Lehmann believes that if the primal story of Cain and Abel, along with its contemporary retelling, dictates our understanding of political beginnings, then the connection between revolution and humanization is forever lost. Crime, not freedom, and violence, not humanizing social cohesion, define the political order. According to Lehmann, "the primal story is indeed too great to be borne" (*Transfiguration,* p. 12).[30] We must, however, recognize its descriptive truth. Lehmann points to the treatment of the American Indian and the black slave as examples of how "civilized" America had its origins in crime and violence.[31]

Although the primal story of violent beginnings can never

---

29. Ibid., p. 83.

30. According to Lehmann, this story has "lingered in the minds and memories of people and hovered over their deeds as a sign of the curse upon the human race as a whole" (*The Transfiguration of Politics,* p. 12).

31. Lehmann, "The Indian Situation as a Question of Accountability," pp. 51-67.

be dismissed entirely, Lehmann believes that another story, the messianic story (a "saving story" with a sense of transcendence), provides the connection between revolution and humanization. The "saving story" arises from the conversation between the Bible and the contemporary situation. As we have seen, the story describes God's presence in human affairs as exerting constant pressure against existing structures to create the "space" necessary for humanization to occur. Accordingly, the self-justifying abuse of power by the existing stories is deemed idolatry (*Transfiguration*, p. 239). In offering this challenge, the "saving story" stands on the side of the *revolutionary* challenge to the existing authorities.

The messianic story serves to invert the political priorities of the existing authorities and to alter the role of violence in revolutionary activity (*Transfiguration*, p. 239). Lehmann first outlines the reversal of political priorities in the existing system and then turns to a discussion of revolutionary violence.

The first reversal in political priorities lies in the affirmation that "freedom is the presupposition and the condition of order: order is not the presupposition and condition of freedom." Lehmann reminds us that the "law and order" position represented by conservative politics in America has always understood chaos as the first enemy of humanity and order as the first priority for human society. Lehmann says that such a position does not represent the biblical understanding of creation. The world itself, Lehmann says, is a product of God's freedom, which pushed back chaos (*Transfiguration*, pp. 240-41):

> It is this electing action of the Creator toward the creation that gives foundational priority to freedom over order, purpose over policy, future over past, and destiny over devices, in the world of time and space and things, and of people in community and in their privacy. (*Transfiguration*, p. 241)

Lehmann believes that the freedom brought into being by God's act of creation indicates that the very "givenness of things" includes within it a "radical permissiveness" (*Transfiguration*, pp. 241-42), which means that God's act of creation demands our freedom to be who we were created to be. When order is given priority over freedom, the result is political abuse of power that denies people the freedom to fulfill their vocation in the world as creatures of God.

According to Lehmann, freedom includes, on the one hand, the celebration of the goodness of things in themselves, the goodness of creation. On the other hand, it includes the "liberating limit" through which the purposes of God direct all living things to their appointed vocations. The biblical description of humanization requires that being free and being bound stand in paradoxical tension (*Transfiguration*, p. 242). Within that paradox, however, freedom takes priority. Freedom celebrates the purpose and diversity of all things, but especially the purpose and diversity of human life. When order is given priority over freedom, it supports the self-justifying power of the establishment, which exchanges the "celebration of difference" for the "power of preference." When order is second to freedom, however, order indicates that one lives "in one time and place" in such a way that one does not "destroy the possibility of other times and places" (*Transfiguration*, pp. 243, 234).

The second reversal has to do with Lehmann's understanding of accountability. Although he refuses to write theological ethics in order to serve what Robin Lovin and others call "public" accountability, for him the concept of "accountability" does constitute a significant aspect of communal life. In his ethics it has nothing to do with searching for a common ground such as human reason on which Christians can persuade non-Christians of the reasonableness of the Christians' ethical stance. Rather, accountability has to do with reciprocal gratitude for the diversity of gifts in God's created order and reciprocal responsibility for human life. The "pattern" that Lehmann identifies points to the order of "liberation, justice, and reconciliation" among human beings.[32]

32. Lehmann, "The Indian Situation as a Question of Accountability," pp. 63ff. It is interesting to note that Lehmann spoke about this pattern of accountability in one of his early articles entitled "The Foundation and

According to this pattern, justice is the key concept, "the link between liberation and reconciliation in the aspiration towards and the achievement of human community."[33] Lehmann believes that God's presence in the human story through the story of Christ's life, death, and destiny alters the meaning of justice as it is usually defined in Western society. Justice is not, he says, adequately defined as *suum cuique,* "to each his own." It is not adequately defined by the understanding of guaranteeing the individual rights of each member of society. When justice is defined in light of the Old Testament understanding of God's righteous will, it points to a *covenantal* rather than a *legal* relation among individuals and groups in society. Living within the context of such a covenant, responsibility for one another takes priority over individual rights. It would be unfair to Lehmann's position, however, to claim that he suggests that oppressed individuals should not fight for their rights before the law. Lehmann's point is that when legal rights are all that bind persons together, the dictates of justice have yet to be filled.

In the pattern of accountability, liberation is listed first because, as explained previously, in freedom resides the very givenness of God's creation. If, however, liberation does not lead to justice, it succumbs to the dangers of ideology, to the "self-justifying self-confidence" that equates God's action with human action. On the other hand, reconciliation without justice is an instance of cheap grace.

When the pattern of liberation, justice, and reconciliation is denied so that the "space" where human life can flourish is experienced instead as a "cramped" condition without freedom, justice, or reconciliation among persons, revolutionary violence often erupts. The question arises, therefore, whether responsible

---

Pattern of Christian Behavior." Here he identified the order as "forgiveness, justice and reconciliation." See "The Foundation and Pattern of Christian Behavior," in *Christian Faith and Social Action,* ed. John A. Hutchison (New York: Charles Scribner's Sons, 1953), pp. 113ff.

33. Lehmann, "The Indian Situation as a Question of Accountability," p. 63.

Christian behavior allows the use of violence in establishing the pattern of accountability.

Lehmann contrasts two views of revolutionary violence by examining the positions of James Cone and Jacques Ellul. Cone forswears pacifism, because, he says, it is dishonest or naive. The pacifistic position, he contends, does not lead one to be truly nonviolent but merely blinds one to the existence of violence. The pacifist can argue against the highly visible, easily recognizable violence of revolutionary activity that uses weapons such as bombs and guns to destroy the existing, unjust government. But Cone believes that pacifism remains naive regarding the systemic violence of society, a violence to which even the pacifist contributes. There are other means for destroying people that are less visible than bombs and guns but equally violent. The pacifist who argues against revolutionary violence but offers no concrete and effective means for resistance against a violent state remains a violent person — that is, a person who, willingly or not, supports a violent system. Cone concludes that one cannot avoid violence. The question for him is not *whether* a person will participate in violence but *which* form of violence one will choose to participate in. This position leads Cone to the justification of revolutionary violence.

Jacques Ellul agrees with Cone that one must acknowledge the systemic presence of violence in society. Violence, he agrees, is not simply produced by picking up a gun. But Ellul disagrees with Cone's argument that the recognition of systemic violence leads to the justification of revolutionary violence. According to Ellul, the Christian is called to break the cycle of violence, not to justify it. Ellul, therefore, heeds Cone's warning against naive pacifism but concludes that Christians cannot justify violence in *any* form (*Transfiguration*, p. 265).

Based on his reading of Cone and Ellul, Lehmann formulates the definition of violence as "the violation of the humanity of my neighbor, by whatever means — military, psychological, moral, medical, institutional, religious." In keeping with his definitions of ethics and the action of God, Lehmann says that "violence is what I do to my neighbor insofar as my involvement makes it impossible for him to be a human being" (*Transfiguration*, p. 265). Lehmann agrees with Cone's insistence that Christians must be aware of the violence of the system in which they live. Because of this systemic violence and the revolutionary counterviolence it provokes, Lehmann does not believe that Christians can accept an unqualified pacifism as an absolute position. Nevertheless, he stands with Ellul and against Cone in claiming that for Christians, violence can never be justified, even when it is aimed at an unjust system. Critics claim that Lehmann is involved in double talk in an attempt to "ride the fence" on the issue of revolutionary violence. Lehmann, however, believes he is describing a genuine "third option" between Cone's justification of violence and Ellul's absolute pacifism.

According to Lehmann, the revolutionary violence that erupts against the corruption, injustice, and violence of society cannot be interpreted as a necessary and therefore justified form of violence. Such revolutionary violence is, however, a *sign* of the "dehumanizing dynamics of the society in which violence has become endemic":

> It is the apocalyptic character of violence that shatters its vicious circle of necessity (contra Ellul) and disallows its justification (contra Cone). Apocalyptically understood, the difference between systemic violence and revolutionary counterviolence is unveiled as the difference between violence that has converted risk into calculated policy and violence as a calculated risk always threatened by conversion into policy. (*Transfiguration*, p. 265)

Lehmann interprets violence as a risk one takes when one sets out to challenge the existing dehumanizing structures. He believes, however, that it can never be a policy or a program. Although one risks involvement in violence, one never thereby justifies violence.

According to Lehmann, the difference between the violence of the oppressive establishment and the violence of the revolutionaries is that the latter is a sign of God's judgment on the former. As a sign of judgment, it is a sign of human brokenness and therefore cannot in itself be glorified or even justified. That Lehmann refuses to allow the risk of violence to become the justification of violence means that he seeks to thwart the programmatic use of violence which makes the revolutionary no different from the establishment (*Transfiguration*, p. 239).

When revolutionary violence is glorified or justified, Lehmann believes that revolution becomes a reign of terror. Arendt points out that revolutionaries do not hesitate to sacrifice persons to principles for the sake of the revolution. Lehmann's fundamental concept of humanization forswears such a turn. Principles, however noble their goal, can never take priority over the humanizing response to persons (*Transfiguration*, p. 6). As Lehmann explains,

> Both revolution and humanization seek to make room for human beings to be free, i.e., seek to establish that stability and security which is required for human beings to treat each other as human beings. Revolution seeks to overthrow the barriers to such humanization. But without a sustaining story revolutions become Reigns of Terror. (*Transfiguration*, p. 7)

To prevent revolutions from "devouring their own children" in a justification of violence, Lehmann believes that revolutions need the saving story of Jesus the Messiah. Only this story sustains the relationship between a new beginning toward freedom and the fulfillment of the promises that the new beginning holds (*Transfiguration*, p. 10). Lehmann falls short, of course, of Lovin's demand for public accountability. Only the community of faith would care what difference the presence of Jesus the Messiah makes to revolutionary activity and revolutionary violence.

Consistent with the fundamental meaning of ethics as reflection on that which holds human society together, Lehmann sets out to describe the ethos, atmosphere, or "space" necessary for making and keeping human life human. His description is grounded in the biblical story of God's action on behalf of creation. He seeks to place the biblical story and biblical images of God's political activity in conversation with the present human story. While the saving story which results from that conversation includes a concern for all humanity, it never abandons its Christian foundations.

Nevertheless, Lehmann, like Barth, does believe that one can translate theological language into language understandable to the world outside the church — hence his frequent references to poetry, philosophy, sociology, and so on. If that translation, however, results in a coincidence of Christian with non-Christian commitment to humanization, that is not evidence of a common rationality, middle axiom, or natural law between them. Rather, it is evidence of the politics of God at work in the world to make and to keep human life human.

Index of Names